INTRODUCTION

Most of us are well aware that what we eat has a direct ~~ ~~
health and fitness. But with so much confusing
know what's healthy and what's not ...

Besides that, we're busy. So, as long as we're n
relegated to the bottom of the priority list. Whc
extent to which the food we eat (or fail to eat)
levels and general well-being.

Since I discovered the impact of food on my he
been on a mission to make it easy for people to ~~eat more~~ healthily. I want to share
what I've learned. And I want to help as many people as possible to make the right
food choices so that they can:

- avoid type 2 diabetes (and in 95% of cases, cure it)
- lower blood pressure and cholesterol
- sleep better and stop snoring
- improve heart and artery health
- feel fitter and have more energy
- enjoy a greater sense of general well-being
- feel sharper all day and avoid afternoon sleepiness, and
- reach their optimal weight.

To this end, I've trained as a nutrition coach (helping over 130 people to get
healthier, fitter and slimmer to date), I speak on nutrition ... and now I've written
this book.

My recipes are based on a few principles. The first is that food should be as delicious
as it is healthy. And then:

- A healthy diet is all about balance, so there's a broad choice of lean meats,
  fish, dairy products, fruit and vegetables, combined with condiments, herbs
  and spices.
- All 100+ recipes are free from added sugars and therefore low-GI (minimum
  alteration of glucose levels).
- All 100+ recipes are made from scratch, with minimal saturated fat and
  processed ingredients.
- You'll be eating wholesome food that's rich in fibre, essential fats, vitamins
  and minerals.
- You won't be eating (and you won't be missing!) refined carbohydrates like
  white bread, white pasta, white rice and, of course, sugar.

ABOUT ME, LEONIE WRIGHT

The turning point for me came a few years ago when I was diagnosed with high cholesterol. I'd already been taking medication for high blood pressure for 14 years and didn't want to take any more. I was fortunate to come across a six-week healthy eating programme in my native Holland and, after completing it, to my delight and amazement, I was able to stop taking my blood pressure medication. My cholesterol level went down and my migraines disappeared.

Prior to that, I'd had no idea that food could have such a huge influence on my health.

The experience inspired me to train as a nutrition coach – so that I could share my knowledge with as many people as possible and give them the support that they need to regain their health. I undertook extensive training both in Holland and in the UK and now run my own practice from home and regularly speak on nutrition.

As I said on the previous page, at the time of writing, I've now helped more than 130 individuals to become healthier, fitter and slimmer through the foods they eat.

Through this book I'm hoping to reach many more!

I hope you'll enjoy it.

If you'd like to know more please take a look at my website at **www.eatwright.co.uk.**

Healthier, fitter and slimmer,
with a lasting result

CONTENTS

To Sharon

With love

Leonie
X.

GLOSSARY

Apple fibre: is made from 100% dried apples and is an excellent source of fibre.

Buckwheat flakes: a great alternative to porridge oats and gluten free.

Chia seeds: is a member of the mint family, a flowering plant and a source of omega-3 fatty acids, dietary fibre, protein, vitamins & minerals. They are neutral in flavour and swell up in water. Can be added to bread, biscuits, smoothies, yoghurt, etc.

Coconut flour: made from dried, ground coconut meat, it has considerable health benefits which far exceed those of processed flours. Just to name a few: it is gluten free, high in fibre, low in carbohydrates, high in beneficial fats, packed with protein and has minimum impact on blood sugar levels hence safe for diabetes patients.

Green Dot: Each recipe has a green dot with the letters B, S, L or D in it. They stand for Breakfast, Snack, Lunch and Dinner; the recommended time of day to eat them.

Herbs: use fresh herbs. If they are not available frozen is an excellent alternative.

Himalayan salt: or pink salt is hand mined from the Himalayan Mountains in Pakistan. It is believed to be the purest salt on earth containing 85.62% sodium chloride and 14.38% trace minerals. It is better than commercial refined salt as it is not stripped of its minerals, not chemically cleaned, bleached and heated at high temperatures. Add it to your food after cooking; this way the minerals will not be destroyed in the cooking process.

Nutritional value: is calculated per person unless otherwise mentioned.

Oil: what oil should you be cooking with? If you know you will be heating olive oil over 130°C/250°F you are running the risk of creating oxidized oil that is harmful to the body. Extra virgin olive oil is a good fat to include in your diet but in a non-heated form such as in salad dressing. However if you use a non-stick frying pan you could put the ingredients in without oil, cook the food on a low temperature, and add the olive oil later. Of all the available oils, coconut oil is the oil of choice for cooking because it is nearly a completely saturated fat, which means it is much less susceptible to heat damage. And coconut oil is one of the most unique and beneficial fats for your body.

Protein powder: preferably use plant protein.

Stevia: is a sweetener and sugar substitute extracted from the leaves of the Stevia plant. It has a negligible effect on the blood sugar level, is 300 times stronger than white refined sugar and has been used for decades in countries like Japan, South America etc. It is available in certain health food stores or can be bought from EatWright. Be aware: most supermarkets sell sweeteners containing a percentage of Stevia however this is not the pure version. In this book I have used the liquid form.

And finally...

I could not have made this book with the help of some wonderful people and a big thank you goes to:

Coby Bouwkamp who has been the inspiration behind the EatWright philosophy, Nigel for lending me his camera, Trevor who gave me a lesson in photography and edited the images, Ozlem and Mara for their input, Fiona, Mike and Mara for proof reading the book, Anne for helping me with the writing and finally Julia Britten from JBS Print & Design (Surrey) Limited for her wonderful design, patience and eye for detail.

CHAPTER 1

BREAKFAST

ALMOND MILK WITH BLUEBERRIES

Serves 1

Nutritional value:

Carbohydrates: 13

Fruit portion: 1

Protein portion: 1½

- 200ml unsweetened almond milk
- 80g blueberries
- 1½ tsp chia seeds
- 15g chopped nuts of your choice
- few drops of pure liquid Stevia

1. Put all the above ingredients in a blender and mix well.

Tip: Add some spices, like ground cinnamon, mixed spice or cloves if you like.

APPLE AND NUTS

The quickest breakfast ever for when you are short of time in the morning!

- 1 apple
- 30g mixed nuts (almonds, walnuts, pecan nuts, Brazil nuts and hazel nuts)

Serves 1

Nutritional value:

Fruit portion: 2

Protein portion: 1

Note:

Nuts are a very healthy protein and rich in energy, packed with antioxidants, vitamins, minerals and omega-3 fatty acids. They are easy to carry around, have a long shelf life and need no preparation. However, be careful with the amount you have, never more than 30g at a time and choose: walnuts, hazel nuts, Brazil nuts, pecan nuts and almonds.

BANANA PANCAKE

This pancake is made without flour and tastes delicious.

Serves 1

Nutritional value:
Carbohydrates: 14
Fruit portion: 1
Protein portion: 1

Tip:
You can add 40g of blueberries to the mixture or replace the banana with 80g of blueberries.

- 1 free range (organic) egg
- 1 small or ½ a large ripe banana
- 1 tbsp desiccated coconut
- 1 tsp olive oil or coconut oil

1. In a bowl mash the banana with a fork.
2. Crack an egg and add to the mashed banana.
3. Beat with a fork until well mixed.
4. Add the desiccated coconut and stir well.
5. Add the olive oil to a small non-stick frying pan and heat on a low setting.
6. Add the banana mixture to the pan and cook, on a low heat, for 3-4 minutes.
7. Turn and cook the second side until golden.

Note:
Make sure the oil is not too hot when you add the banana mixture to avoid burning.

YOGHURT BREAKFAST OPTIONS

BS

Serves 1

Option 1
nutritional value:
Carbohydrates: 17
Fruit portion: 1
Protein portion: 1

Option 2
nutritional value:
Carbohydrates: 12
Protein portion: 1

Option 3
nutritional value:
Carbohydrates: 14
Protein portion: 2

- 200g plain low fat (Greek) yoghurt

Can be mixed with:
- 80g raspberries or
- 80g blueberries or
- 40g raspberries and 40g blueberries or
- 80g strawberries or
- ½ apple with a tsp of cinnamon
- 30g nuts like pecan nuts, Brazil nuts, walnuts, almonds or hazelnuts
- 2 tsp chia seeds or
- 2 tbsp milled flaxseed
- 10g plant based protein powder (optional)

In a bowl mix together the yoghurt with:
1. your choice of fruit and add the chia seeds or flaxseed
2. or the chia seeds and flaxseed
3. or the nuts.

FULL ENGLISH BREAKFAST

Serves 2

Nutrional value:

Carbohydrates: 11

Protein portion: 1½

Vegetable portion: 1½

Did you know:

A full English breakfast does not need to be greasy and fattening as long as you choose the right ingredients. This recipe could also be used for brunch or supper. You can play with the recipe- boil or poach the eggs, and add whatever is in your fridge.

- 6 asparagus spears, trimmed
- 14 vine-ripened baby tomatoes
- 2 portobello mushrooms or 10 medium sized button mushrooms
- 3 free range (organic) eggs
- 1½ tbsp fresh chives, finely cut
- 100g smoked salmon
- freshly ground black pepper and Himalayan salt
- 1 tbsp olive oil

1. Preheat the oven to 180°C/350°F/Gas Mark 4.
2. Clean the asparagus and snap off the tough part of the stalk.
3. Place the asparagus, tomatoes on their vines and the mushrooms on a baking tray.
4. Drizzle with half the olive oil and bake for 20 minutes.
5. Lightly beat the eggs with the chives, and salt and pepper to taste.
6. Heat ½ tbsp of olive oil in a pan.
7. Add the eggs.
8. Cook over a low heat, stirring constantly with a wooden spoon or spatula until almost set.
9. Serve at once with the smoked salmon, asparagus, tomatoes and mushrooms.

LEONIE'S BREAD

I use a bread machine with a nut compartment.

Makes
10-12 slices

Nutritional value
per slice:

Carbohydrates: 13

Grain portion: 1

Note:

I am fifth generation
in a baker's family
and I am very
proud that I have
thought up my very
own recipe!

(Order of putting them into the machine)
- 1 tsp fast-action dried yeast
- 300g organic stoneground strong wholemeal flour
- 75g organic wholegrain Kamut or buckwheat bread flour
- 75g organic stoneground spelt flour
- 1 ¼ tsp Himalayan salt
- 40g extra virgin olive oil
- 315ml cold water

In nut compartment:
- 2 tbsp sunflower seeds
- 1 tbsp pumpkin seeds
- 1 tbsp brown linseed
- 1 tbsp sesame seeds

As there are so many bread machines in the domestic marketplace, it is advisable that the manufacturer's recommended instructions be followed.

To make by hand follow the instructions on the wholemeal flour packet.

PORRIDGE MADE WITH BUCKWHEAT FLAKES

Serves 1

Nutritional value:
Carbohydrates: 9
Protein portion: 1½

- 25g buckwheat flakes or gluten free oats
- 150ml unsweetened almond milk or water
- 15g mixed nuts, chopped
- ½ tsp or more mixed spice or cinnamon
- 1 tsp desiccated coconut

1. Mix the buckwheat flakes or oats with almond milk or water.
2. Add the spice of your choice.
3. Pour mixture into a sauce pan.
4. Bring to the boil, reduce the heat and simmer for 3-4 minutes, stirring occasionally.
5. When ready mix in the nuts and desiccated coconut.
6. Serve with a fruit of your choice.

Tip:
Eat with a fruit portion like a satsuma or your choice of berries.

SCRAMBLED EGGS WITH AVOCADO

Serves 1

Nutritional value:
Carbohydrates: 4
Protein portion: 2

- 2 free range (organic) eggs
- 1 tsp dill or chives, finely chopped
- half an avocado, skin removed and sliced
- Himalayan salt and freshly ground black pepper
- ½ tbsp olive oil

1. Cut the avocado in half lengthwise and twist the 2 halves to separate them.
2. Embed a sharp knife into the stone and pull it out.
3. Lightly score the skin into 2 or 3 strips.
4. Peel off the strips and slice.

To make the scrambled eggs:
1. Lightly beat the eggs with the dill or chives, and add salt and pepper to taste.
2. Heat the olive oil on a low heat in a non-stick frying pan.
3. Add the egg mixture.
4. Cook over a low heat, stirring constantly with a wooden spoon or spatula until almost set.
5. Serve at once with the sliced avocado on the side.

SCRAMBLED EGGS WITH SMOKED SALMON, MUSHROOMS AND TOMATOES

Scrambling eggs takes only minutes – but remember to cook them over a very low heat and to stir them constantly. You can also add different herbs like dill or chives.

Serves 1

Nutritional value:
Carbohydrates: 7
Protein portion: 2½
Vegetable portion: 1

- 2 free range (organic) eggs
- 75g smoked salmon
- 6 medium size button mushrooms
- 1 medium sized tomato, cut in half
- ground black pepper and Himalayan salt
- 2 tbsp olive oil

1. Heat 1 tbsp of olive oil in a small frying pan.
2. Add the whole mushrooms and the two tomato halves.
3. Fry for 6-7 minutes until cooked.

To make the scrambled eggs:
1. Lightly beat the eggs with salt and pepper to taste.
2. Heat 1 tbsp of olive oil in a non-stick frying pan.
3. Add the eggs.
4. Cook over a low heat, stirring constantly and gently with a wooden spoon or spatula until almost set.
5. Serve at once with the salmon, tomatoes and mushrooms.

TWO HARD-BOILED EGGS WITH MUSTARD

Serves 1

Nutritional value:

Protein portion: 2

Note:

Boiling an egg that is perfect, is quite a challenge. Therefore, I wanted to share my method with you.

- 2 free range (organic) eggs
- 1 tsp of mustard of your choice

1. Place the eggs into a saucepan that is the right size so that the eggs sit comfortably and don't crash into one another and cover with cold water.

2. Bring the water up to boiling point then turn to a simmer, put a timer on for 6 minutes if you like them a bit squidgy in the centre, 7 minutes if you like them cooked through.

3. As soon as they are cooked drain off the hot water.

4. Then, the most important part is to cool them rapidly under cold running water. Let the cold water run over them for about a minute, then leave them in cold water until they're cool enough to handle – about 2 minutes. This rapid cooling helps to prevent dark rings forming between the yolk and the white.

5. To peel them, crack the shells all over on a hard surface. Then peel the shell off starting at the wide end.

6. After peeling, rinse again in case there are pieces of shell still clinging.

7. Cut the eggs in bite size parts and dip in the mustard.

A SLICE OF
WHOLEMEAL BREAD

BSL

Serves 1

Nutritional value:

Carbohydrates: 13,
plus 6 for nut butter

Protein portion: 1
(cheese, nut butter
and per egg)

- 1 slice of wholemeal bread served with one of the following:
- 60g low fat cheese or
- 1-2 boiled, poached or scrambled eggs or
- a nut butter (for example, almond butter, hazelnut butter or walnut butter)

CHAPTER 2

SNACKS & SAUCES

APPLE & WALNUT CAKE

Serves 8

Nutritional value
per slice:
Carbohydrates 2½
Protein portion: 0,9

Tip:
Garnish with a
tbsp of quark.

- 200g soya yoghurt
- 40g plant based protein powder
- 3 large free range (organic) eggs
- 1 apple, peeled, cored and sliced
- 2 tbsp buckwheat flakes
- a pinch of Himalayan salt
- 2 tsp baking powder
- 2 tsp ground cinnamon
- pure liquid Stevia
- a few drops of vanilla essence
- 30g walnuts, finely chopped
- 2 tbsp crushed almond flakes, optional
- muffin tray or any other cake tin (20cm round)
- 1 tsp unsalted butter or olive oil

1. Preheat the oven to 180°C/350°F/Gas mark 4.
2. Grease the cake tin or muffin tray with the butter or the oil.
3. Mix the sliced apple with the chopped walnuts, cinnamon, vanilla essence and a few drops of Stevia to taste. Leave to rest.
4. Mix the soya yoghurt with the eggs, protein powder, buckwheat flakes, salt, baking powder, 10 drops of Stevia and a few drops of vanilla essence to a smooth dough.
5. Spoon a layer of the dough mix into the cake tin or muffin tray followed by a layer of the apple mixture and repeat until the dough and apple mixture are finished.
6. Cover the cake with the crushed almond flakes.
7. Bake in the oven for 30-40 minutes or until golden.

BUDWIG PORRIDGE

Serves 1

Nutritional value:

Protein portion: 1

Carbohydrates: 8 for the quark or yoghurt and 4 for the fibre

- 200g quark, low fat natural yoghurt or plain soya yoghurt
- 1 tbsp hazelnut oil or flaxseed oil
- 2 tbsp fibre of your choice i.e. buckwheat flakes, flaxseed
- few drops pure liquid Stevia if you wish

1. Mix/blend all the ingredients together until a smooth consistency.

Tip:
You can also divide the bread mixture over two pound loaf tins and cut it in slices.

CHIA NUT BREAD

BS

Makes 16 slices

Nutritional value per slice:
Carbohydrates: 6
Protein portion: 1

- 100g organic chia seed
- 60g buckwheat flakes
- 120g apple fibre
- 500ml soya yoghurt (or low fat yoghurt or quark)
- 6 large free range (organic) eggs
- 60g mixed nuts (coarsely chopped)
- 40g plant based protein powder
- 12g mixed spice
- pinch of Himalayan salt
- pure liquid Stevia (around 1 tbsp)
- 4 tbsp hazelnut oil
- 20g baking powder

1. Pre-heat the oven to 160°C/325°F/Gas mark 3.
2. Grease a 24cm round tin with a little hazelnut oil.
3. Start by whisking the eggs until light and fluffy.
4. Add all the remaining ingredients to the whisked eggs and beat until well blended.
5. Pour the bread mixture into the tin.
6. Place in the oven and cook for 60 minutes or until firm to touch. A fine skewer inserted into the middle of the bread should come out clean.
7. Leave the bread to cool in the tin for a few minutes, then turn out on to a wire rack and leave to cool completely.
8. Cut the bread in 16 slices, wrap them separately in kitchen foil and freeze.
9. Or you can store the bread in an airtight container in the fridge for a week.

COCONUT TREAT

Makes about 10

Nutritional value per treat:
Protein portion: ⅓

Do not eat more than 2 coconut treats a day as they are high in saturated fat.

- 40g desiccated coconut
- 12g plant based protein powder
- 60ml coconut milk
- 15 drops pure liquid Stevia
- 1 tsp cocoa powder

1. In a large bowl, mix all the ingredients together.
2. Place the mixture in the fridge to cool as it will be easier to handle.
3. Once cooled, divide the mixture into 10 equal parts and roll into little balls.
4. Use a little more desiccated coconut and cover the balls in the coconut by rolling them around.
5. Eat the coconut treat at room temperature but store them in the fridge.

S

Serves 4

Nutritional value
per 50g:
Carbohydrates: 2
Protein portion: ¼
Vegetable portion: 1

GARLIC & CHIVE DIP

- 200g cottage cheese
- 2-3 garlic cloves, crushed (more or less to your taste)
- Himalayan salt and ground black pepper
- fresh chives, cut in 2cm pieces
- 1 tsp lemon juice
- 1 tbsp olive oil
- 5-10 drops pure liquid Stevia
- 100g mix of raw vegetables of your choice, cut into bite size pieces

1. Spoon the cottage cheese into a high beaker, bowl or food processor.
2. Add garlic, salt, pepper, chives, lemon juice, olive oil, and sweetener to taste.
3. Blend with a hand blender or mix in the food processor until it has the consistency of a sauce.
4. Serve as a dip with the raw vegetables.

Tips: • You can make the sauce thinner by adding low fat natural yoghurt. However you might have to add more of the ingredients to keep the taste.
  • If you like, you can also add other ingredients of your choice.
  • This sauce can also be used as a base for a salad dressing, stirred through cooked spinach or served as a barbecue sauce as it goes well with fish or meat.

FIBRE BISCUITS

Makes 4

Tips:

• Make 8 smaller biscuits of 25g (they will be thinner).

• Divide the 200g dough into 20 portions of 10g and bake in a preheated oven for 10-12 minutes.

• The basic recipe makes thin biscuits (similar to crackers).

BASIC RECIPE

- 40g coconut flour
- 10g apple fibre
- 10g desiccated coconut
- 10g organic chia seeds
- 10g plant based protein powder
- 2 large free range (organic) eggs
- 3 tbsp olive oil
- pinch of Himalayan salt

1. Preheat the oven to 150°C/300°F/Gas mark 2.
2. In a large bowl mix all the ingredients and knead until blended.
3. Divide the 200g dough into 4 portions of 50g and either bake:
   - In a waffle iron for about 1 to 2 minutes, or
   - In the oven by rolling each 50g portion into a large biscuit and baking between 10-30 minutes depending on the oven.
4. Store the fibre biscuits in an airtight container in the fridge.

COCONUT/CINNAMON BISCUITS

S

Makes 20

Nutritional value per biscuit:

Carbohydrates: 1

Protein portion: ¼

- 40g coconut flour
- 20g desiccated coconut
- 10g chia seed
- 10g apple fibre
- 2 large free range (organic) eggs
- 2 tbsp olive oil
- 2 tbsp coconut milk
- 1 tsp organic cinnamon
- pure liquid Stevia (3-5 drops) as required

1. Pre-heat the oven to 150°C/300°F/Gas mark 2.
2. In a large bowl mix all the ingredients and knead until blended. The dough will weigh around 200g.
3. Divide the dough into 10g portions, roll out until ½cm and bake in the oven for 10-20 minutes depending on the oven.

ALMOND BISCUITS

Makes 20

Nutritional value
per biscuit:

Carbohydrates: 1
Protein portion: ¼

- 40g coconut flour
- 20g chopped almonds
- 10g chia seed
- 10g apple fibre
- 2 large free range (organic) eggs
- 2 tbsp olive oil
- 1 tbsp hazelnut oil
- pinch of Himalayan salt
- 1 tsp organic cinnamon
- pure liquid Stevia (3-5 drops) as required

1. Pre-heat the oven to 150°C/300°F/Gas mark 2.
1. In a large bowl mix all the ingredients and knead until blended. The dough will weigh around 200g.
1. Divide the dough into 10g portions, roll out until ½cm and bake in the oven for 10-20 minutes depending on the oven.

FISH PATÉ

Serves 2

Nutritional value :

Carbohydrates: 5,
plus 13 if eaten with
oat cakes, crackers
or bread

Protein portion: 1

- 100g tinned tuna in spring water, tinned salmon in olive oil and tinned mackerel or 175g smoked trout or 175g smoked mackerel
- 60g cottage cheese
- 1½ tbsp freshly squeezed lemon juice
- freshly ground black pepper and Himalayan salt

1. When using smoked trout or mackerel: remove the skin and bones. When using tinned tuna, salmon or mackerel remove from the tin.

2. In a food processor or with a hand blender, purée the fish with the cottage cheese, lemon juice and salt and pepper to taste until smooth and well blended.

3. Turn into a bowl and serve with oat cakes, wholemeal crackers or a slice of wholemeal bread.

Tip:

For a coarser consistency you can use a fork instead of a blender.

FRESH OR FROZEN FRUIT MILK SHAKE

SL

Serves 1

Nutritional value:
Carbohydrates:
count the carbs
of the chosen fruit,
berries are 5
Fruit portion: 1
Protein portion: 1

- 200ml unsweetened soya milk, coconut milk or low fat natural yoghurt
- 80g frozen or fresh fruits such as fruits of the forest, raspberries, strawberries, blueberries, melon, banana etc.
- 10-15 drops pure liquid Stevia
- optional: a few drops of fresh lemon juice

You will need a hand blender or food processor

1. Pour the soya milk, coconut milk or low fat natural yoghurt into a high beaker.
2. Add the frozen or fresh fruits, the Stevia and blend.
3. Add fresh lemon to taste or more Stevia if you want.

LUXURY GARLIC SAUCE

Serves 2

Nutritional value:
Carbohydrates: 5
Protein: ⅓

- 125g Greek yogurt (0% fat)
- 2 small red onions, finely chopped
- 1-2 garlic cloves, crushed
- freshly ground black pepper
- 1-2 tsp Provencal herbs
- few drops pure liquid Stevia

1. In a small bowl mix all the ingredients together with a small spoon.

Tip:
Serve with meat. Goes very well with chicken nuggets (p61) or spicy chicken (p64).

GUACAMOLE

Serves 2

Nutritional value:

Carbohydrates: 5

Vegetable portion: 1

Tip:

Traditionally guacamole is served during a Mexican meal but it can also be enjoyed as a tasty dip with oat cakes, wholemeal crackers or crudités.

- 1 large ripe avocado
- ¼ small red onion, finely chopped
- juice of half a lime
- 1 tbsp finely chopped fresh coriander

1. Cut the avocado in half lengthwise and twist the 2 halves to separate them.
2. Embed a sharp knife into the stone and pull it out.
3. Scoop the flesh out with a teaspoon and put in a bowl.
4. Roughly mash with a fork or use a (hand) blender.
5. Add the onion, lime juice and coriander and mix well.
6. Keep in an airtight container in the fridge.

HEALTHY CRÈME FRAÎCHE

Serves 4

Nutritional value:

Carbohydrates: 8

Protein portion: 1

- 200g Cottage cheese
- 3 tbsp water

1. Mix the cottage cheese with the water and blend until smooth. Add a little more water if you need.

2. You can either use a blender or a whisk.

3. This crème fraîche can be refrigerated for a few days as long as no other ingredients have been added.

GREEN PESTO

Serves 2

Nutritional value:
Carbohydrates: 2
Vegetable portion: ½

- 3 handfuls of fresh basil
- 1 garlic clove
- 1-4 tbsp extra virgin olive oil
- 1 tsp freshly squeezed lemon juice
- freshly ground black pepper and Himalayan salt

1. Combine all the above ingredients, except the olive oil, in a food processor or hand blender and mix together until you have a thick paste.
2. Gradually add the olive oil, with the blades turning, scraping the side of the bowl occasionally with a spatula to ensure that all the mixture is incorporated.
3. Add salt and pepper to taste.

HUMMUS

Serves 4

Nutritional value:

Carbohydrates: 16

Vegetable portion: 1

Tip:

• Serve with wholemeal oat cakes, crackers or raw vegetables like cucumber, carrots peppers etc.

• Change the cumin for 1 tsp ground coriander and add a large bunch of fresh, finely cut coriander.

- 400g can chick peas, drained and washed
- 4 tbsp extra virgin olive oil
- 2 tbsp water
- 1-2 garlic cloves, crushed
- juice of 1 lemon
- 1-2 tbsp tahini
- 1 tsp (or a little more) ground cumin
- 1 tsp Himalayan salt

1. In a food processor or with a hand blender, combine the chick peas, olive oil, water, garlic, lemon juice and tahini.
2. Blend until smooth and well mixed.
3. If it appears thick and difficult to blend, add a little more olive oil or water.
4. Season with the salt and cumin.
5. Refrigerate until required.

MAYONNAISE

LD

- 1 free range (organic) egg, at room temperature
- 250ml extra virgin olive oil, groundnut, hazelnut or walnut oil
- 1 tbsp vinegar (e.g. apple cider or white wine vinegar) at room temperature
- Himalayan salt and freshly ground black pepper

1. **Balloon whisk:** Take a bowl and add the egg, salt and pepper to taste and beat together with a balloon whisk until the egg has thickened slightly. Whisk in the oil, just a drop at a time at first, whisking until the mixture is thick. Stir in the vinegar and serve at once or chill.

2. **Blender:** Place the egg, salt and pepper to taste in the bowl of a food processor or blender. Process briefly to combine. With the blades turning, gradually add the oil, pouring it through the funnel in a low, continuous stream.

3. If the mixture doesn't blend it could be that one of the ingredients is too cold.

4. Transfer the mayonnaise to a glass pot with a lid. It can be kept in the fridge provided no other ingredients like mustard, lemon or quark have been added.

MINT SAUCE

Serves 4

Nutritional value:

Carbohydrates: 2

Protein portion: ¼

Vegetable portion: ¼

- 1 tbsp balsamic vinegar
- 50g cucumber, cut in small cubes
- 100g Greek yoghurt (0% fat)
- 1 tsp chopped fresh mint
- 1 tbsp olive oil

1. In a small bowl mix together the balsamic vinegar, cucumber cubes, yoghurt, mint and the olive oil and keep refrigerated.

SPICY APPLE WITH YOGHURT OR CRÈME FRAÎCHE

Serves 2

Nutritional value:
Carbohydrates: 12
Fruit portion: 1
Protein portion: ½

- 300g cooking or eating apples, peeled and cut into cubes
- ½ tsp pure liquid Stevia (if required)
- 1 level tsp ground cinnamon
- ¼ tsp ground cloves
- 2 tbsp water, if needed
- 200g low fat natural yoghurt or low fat crème fraîche

1. Place the apples, spices and Stevia (if using), in a saucepan.
2. Sprinkle with the water, then cook gently until the apples are soft and fluffy.
3. Spoon the mixture into bowls and serve with yoghurt or crème fraîche.

Tip: Mix the yoghurt or crème fraîche with the seeds of 1 vanilla pod.

TOMATO KETCHUP

Nutritional value
for 1 tbsp:

Carbohydrates: 3

- 1x 400g tin organic chopped tomatoes
- 150g onion, finely chopped
- ½ large red pepper, cored, seeded and cut into small pieces
- 1 garlic clove, crushed
- 3 tbsp balsamic vinegar
- 1 tbsp olive oil
- pure liquid Stevia

1. Gently heat the olive oil in a pan.
2. Add the onion, red pepper and garlic and cook gently for 3-4 minutes, stirring from time to time, until soft but not coloured.
3. Add the tomatoes and balsamic vinegar, bring to a boil. Cover and simmer for 3 minutes.
4. Purée the tomato mixture in a food processor until smooth or use a hand blender.
5. Leave the ketchup to cool and add Stevia to taste.
6. Store in the fridge.

WALNUT AND RED PEPPER PASTE DIP

This recipe is courtesy of my dear friend Ozlem from Ozlem's Turkish Table. It is delicious and very more-ish. You can keep the dip covered in the fridge for 3-4 days.

Serves 4–6

Nutritional value:
Carbohydrates: 8
Protein portion: 1¼
Vegetable portion: ½

- 4-5 wholemeal oatcakes weighing about 50g
- ⅓ of a yellow onion (or less), finely chopped
- 3 tbsp (Turkish) red pepper paste (or 1½ tbsp chilli paste)
- ½ tbsp concentrated tomato paste
- 225g walnuts, shelled
- 2 tsp ground cumin
- pinch of Himalayan salt
- 4 tbsp extra virgin olive oil
- 1 tbsp water

1. Grind the walnuts with the onion, cumin, salt and red pepper and tomato paste in a food processor.
2. Soak the oatcakes in water for 1-2 minutes and squeeze out the excess water.
3. Add the oatcakes to the walnut mixture in the food processor.
4. Add the olive oil and water and blend to make a smooth spread. If it appears too thick, add a little more olive oil.
5. Serve with wholemeal oatcakes, crackers or pitta bread.

If you want to make your own red pepper paste please go to Ozlem's website:
www.ozlemsturkishtable.com

YOGHURT AND CHEESE SCONES

SL

Makes 15 pieces
and serves 4 to 6

Nutritional value
per scone:

Carbohydrates: 0.2
Protein portion: ½

- 1 large free range (organic) egg
- 100ml low fat Greek yoghurt (0% fat)
- 1 tsp baking powder
- 10g coconut or almond flour
- 12g plant based protein powder
- 100g Emmental cheese or any other mature cheese, grated
- Himalayan salt and freshly ground black pepper
- assorted seeds like pumpkin, caraway, flaxseed, sesame seeds

1. Preheat the oven to 180°C/350°F/Gas mark 4.
2. Line a baking tray with parchment paper.
3. In a large bowl whisk the egg with the yoghurt.
4. Add the baking powder, flour, plant based protein powder, a pinch of salt and pepper and the grated cheese.
5. When the batter is smooth, drop 15 scoops of the batter onto the baking sheet.
6. Sprinkle the buns with the seeds and bake them for 15 minutes or until lightly golden.
7. Leave to cool and serve.

CHAPTER 3

FISH

COD PARCELS

LD

Serves 4

Nutritional value:
Carbohydrates:
3 per 100g
Protein portion: 1
Vegetable portion: ¾

- 4 x 150g cod fillets
- 150g leeks, cut into thin rings
- ½ large orange or red pepper, cored, seeded and finely chopped
- ½ large yellow pepper, cored, seeded and finely chopped
- 2 spring onions, thinly sliced
- 1 red chilli, cored, seeded and finely chopped

- Himalayan salt and freshly ground black pepper
- 2 tbsp extra virgin olive oil
- baking parchment or kitchen foil

For the tomato sauce:
- 4 tbsp tomato purée
- 4 tbsp fresh basil leaves, finely cut
- 2 tbsp dried Italian herbs

1. Preheat the oven to 220°C/450°F/Gas mark 8.
2. Make the tomato sauce: in a small bowl mix together the tomato purée, basil and Italian herbs.
3. Cut 4 pieces of baking parchment or kitchen foil.
4. Dry the cod fillets with kitchen towel and place each one on a piece of baking paper or kitchen foil.
5. Spread 2 tbsp of tomato sauce on each fillet.
6. Cover each fillet with a quarter of the leeks, pepper, spring onions and the red chilli.
7. Drizzle with a little olive oil.
8. Add Himalayan salt and black pepper to taste.
9. Close the baking parchment/foil to make a parcel.
10. Place the parcels onto a baking tray and bake in the oven for 10-15 minutes until cooked.

Tips:
- If you are short of time you can also use a bag of pre-cut stir-fry vegetables instead of cutting your own.
- The parcels are ideal for heating on the barbecue as well.

LD

Serves 4

Nutritional value:
Carbohydrates: 8
Protein portion: 2
Vegetable portion: 1

COD WITH EGG AND ASPARAGUS

- 400g cod fillet
- 1 clove of garlic, skin removed and cut in half
- 3 tbsp olive oil
- Himalayan salt and freshly ground black pepper
- 600g asparagus
- 4 free range (organic) eggs
- ½ a bunch of tarragon, stems removed and finely cut

1. Heat the oven to 150°C/300°F/Gas mark 2.
2. Rub the cod fillets with the garlic, 2 tbsp olive oil and a little salt and pepper.
3. Place the fillets in a baking dish and bake in the oven for 15 minutes or until cooked.
4. Clean the asparagus and snap off the tough part of the stalk.
5. Bring a large pan of water to the boil and cook the asparagus for 2 minutes until tender.
6. Cool the asparagus in cold water to stop them from cooking further.
7. Poach or boil the eggs.
8. Heat 1 tbsp of olive oil in a frying pan, add the tarragon and asparagus and fry on a low heat for 2 minutes.
9. Season with salt and pepper.
10. Divide the asparagus and cod over 4 plates and serve the egg on top.

COD WITH CELERIAC SPAGHETTI

Serves 4

Nutritional value:
Carbohydrates: 6
Protein portion: 1
Vegetable portion: 1

- 2 tomatoes
- 2 garlic cloves, crushed
- 1 tbsp balsamic vinegar
- 1 tbsp fresh thyme
- leaves of one rosemary sprig, finely chopped
- 4 pieces of cod (approx. 100g each)
- 1 celeriac (about 900g)
- juice of 1 lemon
- 2 tbsp olive oil
- freshly ground black pepper and Himalayan salt
- 3 tbsp chopped fresh, flat-leaf parsley

1. Pre-heat the oven to 200°C/400°F/Gas mark 6.
2. Take the tomatoes, score a cross on top of the tomatoes and immerse in boiling water. Leave for 4-5 minutes, remove from the water and take the skin off.
3. Quarter the tomatoes and discard the pips.
4. Mix the garlic, balsamic vinegar, thyme leaves, rosemary, pepper, salt and 1 tbsp of olive oil in a bowl.
5. Arrange the fish in an oven-proof dish and spread the herb mixture over the fish.
6. Lay the tomatoes on top and sprinkle with half the lemon juice.
7. Bake in the oven for 25 minutes or until cooked.

In the meantime prepare the spaghetti

1. Peel the celeriac and cut with a large kitchen knife into 1½cm slices.
2. Cut each slice into ½cm wide strips.
3. Sprinkle with the left over lemon juice.
4. Blanche the celeriac for 3 minutes in boiling water.
5. Drain the strips in a colander and dry with a clean tea towel.
6. Heat 1 tbsp of olive oil in a frying pan, add the celeriac strips and cook, stirring, until golden brown. Add salt and pepper to taste.
7. On a plate serve a piece of cod with a quarter of the celeriac strips.
8. Pour the left over juice from the oven cooked fish over both and sprinkle with the parsley.

Serve with a nice green salad or French beans

COD WITH SPICY TOMATO SAUCE

LD

Serves 4

Nutritional value:

Carbohydrates: 6

Protein portion: 1½

Vegetable portion: 1

- 4 pieces of cod weighing 100g each
- 4 tomatoes cut into cubes
- 3 tbsp tomato purée
- 1 tsp soy sauce (unsweetened)
- 1 garlic clove, crushed
- 1 small red pepper, cored, seeded and finely chopped
- 3 tbsp olive oil
- Himalayan salt and freshly ground black pepper
- 50ml water

1. First make the tomato sauce by heating 1 tbsp of olive oil in a heavy based frying pan on a low heat.
2. Add the crushed garlic and the tomatoes. Cook for a couple of minutes and add the tomato purée, soy sauce and red pepper.
3. Cover and cook for 15-20 minutes.
4. Stir every now and then. If the sauce becomes too thick add a little bit of water. Take care not to put too much water in!
5. Dry the fish with kitchen towel.
6. Brush the fish with the rest of the olive oil and season.
7. Heat a non-stick frying pan, add the cod and cook for 3 minutes on each side until the fish is opaque and the flesh nearly flakes.
8. Serve the fish and sauce on heated plates.

COURGETTE FRITTERS WITH SALMON

SLD

Serves 4

Nutritional value per fritter:

Carbohydrates: 1½

Protein portion: ¼

Vegetable portion: ¼

Tips:

• You can easily take these fritters with you in an airtight container with some kitchen towel on the bottom.

• Store the fritters in an airtight container in the fridge.

- 1 courgette, grated
- 1 free range (organic) egg
- 10g plant based protein powder
- 50g smoked salmon, cut into small pieces
- 2 tbsp finely chopped mint leaves
- 5 tbsp olive oil
- 100g low fat natural yoghurt
- freshly ground black pepper and Himalayan salt

1. Dry the grated courgette with paper towels.
2. Whisk the egg with the protein powder and add salt and pepper to taste.
3. Mix the courgette, salmon and ¾ of the mint leaves through the egg mixture.
4. Heat the olive oil in a frying pan and spoon 6 little heaps of the mixture into the pan.
5. Press flat with the round side of a spoon and fry on a high setting for 4-6 minutes until brown on both sides.
6. Once cooked lift the fritters out of the pan and drain on paper towels.
7. Make another 6 fritters with the rest of the mixture.
8. For the dip, mix the yoghurt with the rest of the mint and add salt and pepper to taste.

FISH PIE WITH CELERIAC TOPPING

Serves 6

Nutritional value:
Carbohydrates: 10
Protein portion: 1
Vegetable portion: 1½

- 2 x 800g celeriac: peeled and cut into cubes
- Himalayan salt and freshly ground black pepper
- 2 leeks, trimmed and thinly sliced
- 2 cloves of garlic, peeled and finely chopped
- 2 tbsp olive oil
- optional: 100ml dry white wine
- 250ml fish or vegetable stock
- 1 heaped tbsp cornflour
- 2 tbsp low-fat crème fraîche (see p30 for recipe)
- 25g flat leaf parsley, finely chopped
- 200g boneless salmon fillets, cut into 2½cm cubes
- 500g fish pie mix
- 300g raw (king) prawns

1. Put the celeriac into a saucepan, cover with water, bring to the boil and simmer for around 30 minutes or until tender. Drain well, season to taste and mash.

2. Preheat the oven to 190°C/375°F/Gas mark 5 or for a fan oven 170°C/335°F/Gas mark 4.

3. Sweat the leeks and garlic in a deep frying pan with the olive oil for 4 to 5 minutes.

4. Pour in the (optional wine and) stock and simmer for a couple of minutes.

5. Mix the cornflour with 1 tablespoon water and stir into the leek sauce, then add the crème fraîche and parsley.

6. In a separate frying pan, fry the salmon fillets and fish pie mix for about 2 minutes, just to get some colour, or put the fish pie mix and salmon fillets in the microwave on a medium setting for 5 minutes.

7. Stir the salmon, fish pie mix and prawns into the leek sauce.

8. Check the seasoning and poor into a 25 x 20cm shallow baking dish.

9. Top with the celeriac mash and bake for 30 minutes or until golden brown.

FISH STEW

- 400g white fish of your choice
- 200g salmon steaks
- 100g cooked prawns
- 250g chestnut mushrooms, thinly sliced
- 200ml soya milk (unsweetened)
- 2 tbsp cornflour
- freshly ground black pepper and Himalayan salt

- 1 tsp ground nutmeg
- juice of one lemon
- 500ml fish stock (one stock cube)
- 1 celery stick, finely chopped
- 1 leek (white part only), finely chopped
- 3 tbsp flat leaf parsley, finely cut
- 3 tbsp olive oil

1. Pre-heat oven to 160°C/325°F/Gas mark 3
2. Heat 2 tbsp of olive oil in a frying pan, add the leek and celery, fry for 1 minute and set aside.
3. Make the fish stock and poach the salmon and white fish in the stock until cooked.
4. Lift the fish out of the stock and place in an oven proof dish.
5. Strain the stock and reserve.
6. Heat the remaining olive oil in a frying pan, add the mushrooms and cook for 5 minutes.
7. In a small sauce pan mix the soya milk with 100ml fish stock and heat on a medium heat.
8. Mix the cornflour with 1½ tbsp cold water and add to the soya milk mixture.
9. Simmer until the sauce starts to thicken.
10. Add pepper, salt and nutmeg to taste.
11. Place the fish in an oven proof dish, add the prawns, leeks, celery and mushrooms and cover with the sauce.
12. Bake in the oven for 10 minutes.
13. Drizzle the fish with the lemon juice and garnish with the chopped parsley.

LD

Serves 4

Nutritional value:
Carbohydrates: 2½
Vegetable portion: ½
Protein portion: 1½

BAKED HADDOCK WITH LEEKS

Serves 4

Nutritional value:
Carbohydrates: 3½
Protein portion: 1½
Vegetable portion: ½

- 400g haddock fillets, fresh or frozen
- 300g leeks, washed and thinly sliced
- 1 onion, finely chopped
- 60g grated low fat cheese
- 100ml soya milk (unsweetened)
- 1 tbsp curry or tumeric powder

- 2 tbsp olive oil
- Himalayan salt and freshly ground black pepper

For EatWright crème fraîche:
- 100g cottage cheese
- 2 tbsp water

1. Defrost the fish (if frozen), dry with kitchen towel and season.
2. Preheat the oven to 200°C/400°F/Gas mark 6.
3. Grease an oven proof dish with a little olive oil.
4. Spread the leeks on the bottom of the dish.
5. Heat 1 tbsp of olive oil in a frying pan and on a low heat, fry the onion until softened but not burned.
6. Add the curry or tumeric powder and fry briefly.
7. Heat the rest of the olive oil in a clean frying pan and fry the fish on either side for 1 minute.
8. Place the fish on top of the leeks in the oven dish and divide the onion mixture over it.
9. For the crème fraîche, blend 100g cottage cheese with 2 tbsp of water.
10. Mix the grated cheese, soya milk and crème fraîche and pour over the fish.
11. Bake in the oven for 25 -30 minutes until the fish is cooked and the top is golden and bubbling.

MACKEREL SANDWICH WITH MAYONNAISE

If you do not want to spend too much time in the kitchen here's a solution for a quick lunch or dinner. You do not need to make your own mayonnaise but it does finish it off!

LD

Serves 1

Nutritional value per sandwich:

Carbohydrates: 15

Vegetable portion: ½

Protein portion: 1

Tip:

If you like you can add some capers as well.

- 150g steamed or smoked mackerel
- 1 tbsp mayonnaise (homemade, see p33)
- 1 slice of wholemeal or spelt bread
- 25g fresh spinach or lettuce
- 4 slices of cucumber
- 2 radishes, sliced
- Himalayan salt and freshly ground black pepper

1. Cut the mackerel open and take the meat out with a knife. Watch the bones.
2. Wash and dry the spinach/lettuce and mix with a little mayonnaise.
3. Lay the spinach or lettuce and sliced cucumber on one half of the sandwich. Top this up with the mackerel and radishes and finish it off with the rest of the mayonnaise.
4. Finally add some pepper and salt to taste and put the other half of the sandwich on top.

Tip:
Serve with quick ratatouille or spinach

MUSSELS

Serves 2

Nutritional value:

Carbohydrates: 7

Protein portion: 1

Vegetable potion: 1

- 1kg mussels, cleaned (hold under cold running water and scrub with a small stiff brush. To remove the beard, hold the beard firmly between your thumb and the blade of a small knife and pull the beard away from the shell)
- 1 tbsp olive oil
- 1 small onion, finely chopped
- 3 leeks, washed, trimmed and thinly sliced
- 1 garlic clove, crushed
- 1 bunch of fresh flat leaf parsley, thick stalks removed, finely chopped
- freshly ground black pepper
- optional: 100ml dry white wine

1. Heat the olive oil in a large saucepan with the onion, leeks, garlic and parsley and cook gently, stirring occasionally, for a few minutes until the vegetables are soft but not coloured.
2. Add the pepper and white wine (if using) and stir.
3. Add the mussels, cover the sauce pan tightly and bring to the boil.
4. Cook for 4 minutes, remove the lid and give the mussels a stir.
5. Place the lid back on the saucepan and cook for a further 2 minutes or until the mussels open.
6. Throw away any mussels that have not opened.
7. Transfer the mussels to two plates and pour the leek sauce over the mussels.
8. Serve at once.

OVEN BAKED COD

Serves 1

Nutritional value:
Carbohydrates: 6
Protein portion: 1½

Tip:
Serve with a
green salad or
a vegetable
like broccoli or
green beans.

- 100g cod
- 1 tsp mustard (without sugar)
- 1 tbsp soy sauce (without sugar)
- freshly ground black pepper
- Himalayan salt
- 1 medium size tomato, sliced
- 25g cottage cheese
- 1 tsp plant based protein powder

1. Preheat the oven to 200°C/400°F/Gas mark 6.
2. **To make the sauce:** combine the mustard, soy sauce, pepper and salt.
3. Place the cod into a small oven proof dish, spread the sauce over the cod and bake in the oven for 15 minutes.
4. Take the fish out of the oven.
5. Cover the fish with the sliced tomato
6. Spread the cottage cheese over the tomato and sprinkle with the protein powder for a crispy top.
7. Return to the oven and bake for another 10 minutes.
8. Serve at once.

PRAWN AND VEGETABLE STIR-FRY

Serves 2

Nutritional value:
Carbohydrates: 9½
Protein portion: 1½
Vegetable portion: 1½

- 100g pak choi, washed and shredded
- 100g bean sprouts
- 100g white cabbage, shredded
- 1 large red pepper, cored, deseeded and sliced thinly
- 300g cooked king prawns
- 2 tbsp chopped fresh coriander
- 1 garlic clove, crushed
- 4cm piece of fresh root ginger, peeled and finely chopped
- 2 tbsp olive oil

1. Heat the olive oil in a wok or frying pan, add the ginger and garlic and stir-fry for 2 minutes.
2. Add the cabbage and red pepper and stir-fry for 3-4 minutes until hot.
3. Stir in the bean sprouts and the pak choi.
4. Add the prawns and simmer for a further 3-4 minutes to heat through.
5. Garnish with coriander and serve immediately.

PRAWN STIR-FRY WITH SPINACH

LD

Serves 2

Nutritional value:

Carbohydrates: 7

Protein portion: 1½

Vegetable portion: 1

- 40g Parma ham (no sugar), finely cut
- 1 small red pepper, cored, seeded and finely chopped
- 1 tbsp olive oil
- 200g large raw prawns
- 1 tsp lemon zest
- 300g washed, fresh spinach
- 1-2 tsp cayenne pepper or chilli powder
- 1 small red onion, cut into thin rings

1. Heat the olive oil in a wok or large frying pan, add the Parma ham and the red pepper and stir-fry for 3-4 minutes until crispy.
2. Add the prawns and lemon zest to the wok and stir-fry over a high heat.
3. After 1 minute add the spinach and stir-fry for a further 3-4 minutes on high heat until the spinach has wilted.
4. Finally, add the cayenne pepper or chilli powder to taste and garnish with the red onion.

SALMON WITH TOMATOES AND OLIVES

I love Turkish food mainly because it is tasty and healthy. I was very pleased when my Turkish friend Ozlem introduced me to this recipe. Thank you Ozlem from Ozlem's Turkish Table.

Serves 4

Nutritional value:

Carbohydrates: 8

Protein portion: 1

Vegetable portion: 1½

Tip:

Tastes delicious with samphire (see p102 for recipe).

- 4 salmon fillets, weighing 150g each
- 16-18 cherry tomatoes, halved
- 2 tbsp olives, pitted and halved
- 2 tbsp olive oil
- freshly ground black pepper
- wedges of lemon to serve

1. Preheat the oven to 180°C/350°F/Gas mark 4.
2. Grease a baking tray with the olive oil and place the salmon fillets in it.
3. Spread the cherry tomatoes and olives over and around the salmon fillets and season with ground black pepper.
4. Place the tray in the preheated oven for about 20-25 minutes until the fish is cooked and the tomatoes are starting to turn crisp at the edges.

SEA BASS WITH COURGETTE, TOMATO AND PESTO

LD

Serves 2

Nutritional value:

Carbohydrates: 5
Protein portion: 1
Vegetable portion: 1

- 200g sea bass
- 100g tomatoes, cut in half
- 100g courgette, cut in 1cm slices
- 6-8 fresh basil leaves
- freshly ground black pepper and Himalayan salt
- 1 tbsp extra virgin olive oil

1. Season the sea bass, tomatoes and courgette, add the basil and place on a grill (If you do not have a grill you can use a griddle pan or fry the fish in 1 tbsp of olive oil).
2. After 15 minutes take the sea bass from the grill and keep warm.
3. Grill the tomatoes and courgette further until soft and brown.
4. Make the pesto. For recipe, see page 31.
5. Serve the sea bass with the tomatoes, courgette and the pesto and drizzle with a little olive oil.

THAI FISH STIR-FRY

Serves 2

Nutritional value:
Vegetable portion: 1
Carbohydrates: 5
Protein portion: 1

- 1 tsp tomato purée
- dash of soy sauce (unsweetened)
- 1 tsp sambal (unsweetened) or hot chilli paste
- 1 garlic clove, crushed
- quarter of a pak choi stalk
- 1 small tomato, cut into small cubes
- florets from a quarter of a broccoli head
- dash of olive oil
- 300g salmon fillet, cut into pieces
- dash of lemon juice
- 1 small red onion, finely cut
- pinch of Himalayan salt and freshly ground black pepper

1. Marinate the salmon fillet in the lemon juice, cover and leave in the fridge for a couple of hours.
2. Cut the white part of the pak choi into pieces and tear the green part into bits.
3. It might be a good idea to put all the ingredients in separate bowls.
4. Heat the olive oil in a wok or large frying pan and briefly stir-fry the onion, the white part of the pak choi, the broccoli and the sambal/chilli paste over a medium heat.
5. Add the crushed garlic and salt and pepper to taste.
6. Take the salmon out of the fridge, discard the lemon juice and add to the wok.
7. Stir-fry the salmon until cooked, add the green part of the pak choi and the tomato cubes and stir-fry for 1 minute.
8. Finally add the tomato purée and soy sauce and cook for a further 5 minutes.

CHAPTER 4

POULTRY & GAME

MILD CURRIED CHICKEN WITH YOGHURT

Serves 4

Nutritional value:

Carbohydrates: 4

Protein portion: 1½

Vegetable portion: ½

Tip:

Stir-frying is an excellent way to cook healthily: due to the short preparation time, vitamins will be retained.

- 500g boneless chicken breasts, skinned and cut into 2½cm cubes
- 2 tbsp olive oil
- 2 onions, peeled and finely chopped
- 300g leeks (around 4 leeks) only the white part, thinly sliced
- 200ml low fat plain natural yoghurt (max. 4 carbs for 100ml)
- 2 tbsp Korma curry spices or another mild curry powder
- 1 tbsp finely chopped fresh coriander
- freshly ground black pepper and Himalayan salt

1. Heat the olive oil in a wok or large frying pan, add the onions and stir-fry over a medium heat (be careful not to overheat the oil as it will oxidise).
2. After one minute add the chicken and fry on all sides until brown.
3. Add the leeks and stir-fry for a further 3 minutes until the leeks are soft.
4. Mix the yoghurt with the curry powder and the fresh coriander and stir through the chicken. Cook for a further 4 minutes.
5. Add salt and/or pepper to taste and serve hot.

CHICKEN FILLETS WITH PROSCIUTTO

Serves 4

Nutritional value:

Carbohydrates: 1

Protein portion: 1

Tip:

Goes really well with freshly cooked leeks or French beans.

- 1 garlic clove, finely cut
- 1 onion, finely chopped
- 5cm piece of fresh root ginger, peeled and finely chopped
- 4 boneless chicken breasts, skinned, weighing 100g each
- 2 tbsp soy sauce (unsweetened)
- 8 slices of cured ham without sugar e.g. prosciutto
- 2 tbsp olive oil

1. Preheat the oven at 180°C/350°F/Gas mark 4.
2. Lightly butter or oil an oven proof dish.
3. Heat the olive oil in a frying pan, add the garlic, onion and ginger, and cook gently stirring occasionally, for 5-6 minutes until the onions are softened but not coloured.
4. Flatten the chicken fillets and brush both sides with the soy sauce.
5. Divide the onion mixture over the chicken fillets.
6. Wrap each chicken breast with 2 slices of prosciutto.
7. Place the fillets in the oven proof dish.
8. Bake in the middle of the oven for approximately 25 minutes or until cooked.

LD

Serves 4

Nutritional value:
Carbohydrates: 11
Protein portion: 1½
Vegetable portion: 1½

CHICKEN WITH PEPPERS AND CASHEW NUTS

- 600g boneless chicken breasts, skinned and cut into bite-size pieces
- 150g oyster mushrooms, roughly sliced
- 150g shiitake mushrooms, roughly sliced
- 2 large red peppers, cored, seeded and cut into 2½cm squares
- 1 large onion, cut into 2½cm squares
- 2 tbsp olive oil
- 5cm of fresh ginger, finely chopped

- 2 garlic cloves, finely chopped
- 1 tbsp light soy sauce (unsweetened)
- 85g cashew nuts, roasted
- 3 tbsp mushroom ketchup (optional)
- water if needed

Marinade:
- 3 tbsp light soy sauce (unsweetened)
- 1 tsp Shaoxing rice wine
- 5 drops pure liquid Stevia

1. Combine all the ingredients for the marinade in a bowl and marinate the chicken, covered, for at least 20 minutes.
2. In a preheated wok or deep saucepan, heat 1 tbsp of olive oil. Add the ginger and stir-fry until fragrant. Stir in the chicken and cook for 2 minutes, or until it begins to turn brown. Before the chicken is cooked through, remove and set aside.
3. In the same wok or deep saucepan, heat the remaining oil and stir-fry the garlic until fragrant. Add the onion, red peppers and mushrooms and stir-fry for 2 minutes. Add 3 tbsp of water or the mushroom ketchup and cook for about 4 minutes or until the water/ketchup has evaporated.
4. Return the chicken to the wok, than add the light soy sauce and cashew nuts and stir-fry for 3 minutes or until the chicken is thoroughly cooked through.

CHICKEN OR FISH NUGGETS

Serves 1

Nutritional value:

Protein portion: 2½

Tips:

• This is an ideal snack for when you are travelling.

• Make more and freeze.

- 10g plant based protein powder
- 1 tsp curry powder or any other spice you like
- 1-2 tbsp olive oil
- 150g boneless chicken breasts, skinned, fish or meat of your choice cut into small strips

1. Mix the protein powder with the curry powder or spice of your choice.

2. Toss the chicken, fish or meat strips in the dry marinade, cover, and leave to stand for a few minutes (if you are short of the spice mixture, double the quantity).

3. Heat the olive oil in a wok or large frying pan.

4. Add the chicken, fish or meat and stir-fry over a medium heat and cook for 8-9 minutes or until tender. The chicken, fish or meat will expand a little so make sure you have enough olive oil in your pan. Don't let the olive oil become too hot or it may oxidise and become harmful.

LD

Serves 4

Nutritional value:
Carbohydrates: 9
Protein portion: 1¼
Vegetable portion: 1½

GINGER CHICKEN WITH TOASTED SESAME SEEDS

- 500g boneless chicken breasts, skinned and cut into strips
- 2 tbsp olive oil
- 1 leek, thinly sliced
- 1 head of broccoli, cut into small florets
- 1 large orange pepper, cored, seeded and cut into small squares
- ½ cauliflower, cut into small florets
- 1 tsp grated fresh ginger
- 2 tbsp sesame seeds
- 1 tbsp cornflour
- 1 tbsp water
- 4 tbsp soy sauce (unsweetened)
- 4 tbsp water

1. In a medium dish combine the soy sauce with 4 tbsp of water. Toss and coat the chicken strips in the sauce and cover the dish with cling film. Chill in the fridge for an hour.

2. Remove the chicken from the marinade with a slotted spoon.

3. Heat the oil in a frying pan or wok and stir-fry the chicken and leek until the chicken is browned and the leek is beginning to soften.

4. Stir in the vegetables and ginger. Reduce the heat, cover and simmer for 5 minutes.

5. Place the sesame seeds on a baking sheet under a hot grill. Stir them once to make sure they toast evenly. Set aside to cool.

6. In a small bowl, combine the cornflour with 1 tbsp of water and whisk until smooth. Gradually add the liquid to the frying pan, stirring constantly until thickened.

7. Top with the sesame seeds and serve.

ROAST CHICKEN WITH ROSEMARY AND THYME

Serves 4

Nutritional value :

Carbohydrates: 0

Protein portion:
1 per 100g

- 1 medium size whole fresh organic or free range chicken (weighing about 1.8kg)
- 3 tbsp fresh rosemary, finely chopped
- 2 tbsp fresh thyme, finely chopped
- ½ tsp Himalayan salt
- ¼ tsp freshly ground black pepper
- 1 lemon, cut into quarters
- 1 tbsp olive oil
- 5 garlic cloves, peeled and cut in half

1. Preheat oven to 190°C/375°F/Gas mark 5.
2. Pat the chicken dry with paper towels and lay breast side up in a roasting tin.
3. In a small bowl combine half of the rosemary with half of the thyme, salt and black pepper, set aside.
4. Place the lemon quarters, the remaining rosemary and thyme and the garlic inside the cavity of the chicken.
5. Brush the outside of the chicken with the olive oil and coat completely with the seasoning mixture.
6. Cover with kitchen foil and bake for around 60 minutes.
7. Carefully remove the foil and continue roasting for another 25-30 minutes.
8. Remove the chicken from the roasting tin and leave to stand for 10 minutes before carving.

SPICY CHICKEN

- 200g boneless chicken breasts, skinned and cut into strips
- 100g mushrooms, thinly sliced
- 80g large red pepper, cored, deseeded and cut into strips
- 1 medium size onion, finely chopped
- 2 garlic cloves, crushed (optional)
- 200g cucumber, cut into 1cm cubes
- 1 tbsp olive oil

Dry marinade:

- 2 tbsp ground cumin
- 2 tbsp ground coriander
- 1 tbsp ground cinnamon
- 1 tsp ground nutmeg
- 2 tsp ground paprika
- 1 tsp freshly ground black pepper
- 1 tsp curry powder
- ½ tsp Himalayan salt

1. Make the dry marinade: thoroughly combine cumin, coriander, cinnamon, nutmeg, paprika, black pepper, curry powder and salt in a jug or bowl and shake well. I find that a used, cleaned jam jar works really well for mixing the spices.

2. In a large bowl, toss the chicken strips with as much dry marinade as you like, cover and leave to stand for a few minutes, while you prepare the vegetables. Any left over spice mixture can be kept for future use.

3. Heat the olive oil in a wok or large frying pan, add the chicken and fry over a medium heat for 5-7 minutes until the chicken begins to colour and is tender.

4. Add the mushrooms, pepper, onion and garlic and cook for a further 5 minutes.

5. Serve at once with the cucumber.

Vegetarian tip:

This dish can easily be made into a vegetarian dish by replacing the chicken with tofu.

LD

Serves 2

Nutritional value:
Carbohydrates: 7
Protein portion: 1
Raw vegetable portion: 1
Vegetable portion: 1

STIR-FRIED CHICKEN WITH VEGETABLES

Serves 4

Nutritional value:

Carbohydrates: 5

Vegetable portion: 1

Protein portion: 1

- 3 tbsp olive oil
- 2cm fresh root ginger, finely chopped
- 2 crushed garlic cloves
- 1 large red pepper, cored, deseeded and finely chopped
- 400g boneless chicken breasts, skinned and cut into 5mm strips or cubes
- 2 red onions, cut in half and sliced
- 1 small pak choi cut into strips (±400g)
- 1-2 tbsp soy sauce (unsweetened)
- Himalayan salt and freshly ground black pepper

1. Heat the olive oil in a large pan or wok, add the ginger, garlic and red pepper and stir-fry for 2 minutes
2. Add the chicken strips and stir-fry for another 3-4 minutes.
3. Add the onions and the white, hard parts of the pak choi and stir-fry for 3-4 minutes.
4. Add the green parts of the pak choi and stir-fry on a high heat until the pak choi has wilted.
5. Finally add soy sauce and salt and pepper to taste and heat through for 1-2 minutes.

STUFFED CHICKEN BREAST

Serves 2

Nutritional value:

Carbohydrates: 5

Protein portion: 1¼

Raw vegetable portion: 1

Tip:

Serve with a nice green salad!

- 2 boneless chicken breasts, skinned, weighing approx. 125g each
- 2 tbsp olive oil

For the stuffing:

- 16 black olives, pitted
- 1 garlic clove
- 10 basil leaves
- freshly ground black pepper and Himalayan salt

1. Preheat the oven to 200°C/400°F/Gas mark 6.
2. Put all the ingredients for the stuffing in a food processor or use a hand blender and blend until it resembles a paste.
3. With a sharp kitchen knife make 4 deep cuts in each chicken breast and fill the breast with the stuffing.
4. Heat the olive oil (on a low heat) in a frying pan and fry the chicken breast on both sides until browned.
5. Put both breasts in an oven proof dish and cook for a further 8-10 minutes until ready.

TANDOORI CHICKEN

LD

Serves 4

Nutritional value:

Carbohydrates: 9

Protein portion: 1½

Vegetable portion: 1¼

- 500g boneless chicken breasts, skinned and cut into 2½cm squares
- 2 medium size onions, roughly chopped
- 1 orange and 1 red pepper, cored, seeded and cut into 2½cm squares
- 3 tomatoes, chopped
- 5cm fresh root ginger, finely chopped
- 2 garlic cloves, crushed
- 1 tbsp chilli powder
- 2 tbsp tandoori curry powder
- 1 tsp garam masala
- 150g low fat natural yoghurt

1. Heat the olive oil in a wok or large frying pan.
2. Add the garlic and ginger and stir-fry over a medium heat for 1 minute.
3. Add the onions, peppers, chilli and curry powder and the garam masala, stir and fry for 4 minutes.
4. Add the tomatoes and chicken and cook for 20-25 minutes, stirring occasionally.
5. Finally, add the yoghurt just before serving.

VENISON STEAK WITH BALSAMIC-GARLIC SAUCE

Serves 4

Nutritional value:
Carbohydrates: 2½
Protein portion: 1½
Vegetable portion: ½

- 4 small venison steaks, weighing approx. 150g each
- Himalayan salt and freshly ground black pepper
- 200g oyster mushrooms, wiped clean and cut in half
- 40g unsalted butter
- 1 tbsp olive oil
- 4 shallots, quartered
- 1 garlic clove, thinly sliced
- 2 tbsp balsamic vinegar
- ½ tsp dried thyme
- 150ml beef stock

1. Season the steaks with salt and pepper.
2. Heat the butter and olive oil in a frying pan and fry the steaks for 2-3 minutes on each side.
3. Remove the meat from the pan and keep warm.
4. Add the shallots and garlic to the pan and fry for 3 minutes.
5. Add the balsamic vinegar to the shallots and garlic, to deglaze.
6. Then add the oyster mushrooms and thyme and pour in the stock.
7. Cook the sauce for 2 minutes.
8. If necessary, thicken the sauce by adding 1 tsp cornflour to 2 tsp water.
9. Serve the steaks with the sauce.

CHAPTER 5

MEAT DISHES

AUBERGINE AND MINCE BAKE

Serves 4

Nutritional value:
Carbohydrates: 4
Vegetable portion: 1
Protein portion: 2

- 500g aubergines, washed and cut into 2½cm cubes
- 400g lean (organic) minced beef containing 5% fat or less
- 200g low fat mature Cheddar cheese, grated

1. Heat a non-stick frying pan, add the minced beef and cook, stirring for 5 minutes or until the beef is browned.

2. Add the aubergine cubes and stir-fry until cooked.

3. Sprinkle the grated cheese over the aubergine and mince mixture (you could also use sliced cheese).

4. Put the lid on the pan.

5. Keep checking regularly, the dish is ready when the cheese has melted.

Vegetarian tip:
You can replace the minced beef with minced quorn.

CHINESE CABBAGE WITH MINCE

- 800g Chinese cabbage, washed and leaves separated
- 250g lean (organic) minced beef (5% fat)
- 1 tbsp olive oil
- 2 free range (organic) eggs
- 1 beef or vegetable stock cube
- 2 shallots, finely chopped
- 1½ tsp chilli powder
- 1 tbsp flat leaf parsley, finely chopped
- ½ tsp Himalayan salt
- freshly ground black pepper
- 1 tbsp cornflour

1. Blanch the cabbage in boiling water for 4 minutes until just tender.
2. Drain and roughly cut the leaves, keep warm.
3. Boil the eggs for about 7 minutes. Cool, slice and set aside.
4. Heat the oil in a medium size frying pan and add the shallots and minced beef and cook, stirring, for 5 minutes or until the beef is browned and the onion softened.
5. Add the chilli powder, pepper, salt and the stock cube, and cook, stirring for 2 minutes.
6. If the consistency is too liquid, mix the cornflour with 1 tbsp water and add to the mince mixture.
7. Serve the cabbage on a plate and cover with the mince.
8. Garnish with the sliced egg and chopped parsley.

Note:

Surprisingly tasty!

LD

Serves 4

Nutritional value:
Carbohydrates: 5
Protein portion: 1
Vegetable portion: 1

FILLET STEAK WITH LEMON SPINACH

Serves 2

Nutritional value:

Carbohydrates: 7

Protein portion: 1¾

Vegetable portion: 1

Tip:

This is an amazing quick, easy and nutritious dish full of lovely flavours.

- 2 x 125g fillet steak
- 400g fresh spinach, washed
- 2 garlic cloves, crushed
- grated zest of half a lemon
- 30g almonds, roughly chopped
- Himalayan salt and freshly ground black pepper
- 1 tbsp olive oil

1. Dry the fillet steak with kitchen towel, sprinkle with pepper and fry in a non-stick frying pan, on a medium heat until pink (keep warm).
2. Heat the olive oil in a wok, add the crushed garlic and fry for 30 seconds.
3. Add the spinach bit by bit and stir-fry until wilted.
4. Stir in the lemon zest, salt and pepper to taste, and stir-fry for a minute.
5. Sprinkle with the chopped almonds.
6. Serve the steak on heated plates with the spinach on the side.

This recipe is a different version of the traditional Bolognese sauce containing fresh ingredients and very versatile as you can vary the vegetables you use.

Instead of pasta this dish can be served with cauliflower or salad.

BOLOGNESE SAUCE

LD

Serves 4

Nutritional value:
Carbohydrates: 13
Protein portion: 1¼
Vegetable portion: 1½

To serve:
When using cauliflower break the cauliflower into small pieces or use a food processor. Cook for 1-5 minutes. Cauliflower is also an excellent replacement for rice and couscous either raw or cooked. Here I used iceberg lettuce, tomatoes, cucumber and drizzled it with a little extra virgin olive oil and balsamic vinegar.

- 500g lean (organic) minced beef containing 5% fat
- 2 tbsp olive oil
- 2 large onions, finely cut
- 2 garlic cloves, crushed
- 2 medium size carrots, thinly sliced
- 2 celery sticks, thinly sliced
- 1 red pepper, cored, seeded and chopped into small squares
- 1 green pepper, cored, seeded and chopped into small squares.
- 400g tin of organic chopped tomatoes
- 3 tbsp tomato purée
- ½ tube of sun-dried tomato paste
- 1 tbsp dried oregano
- 1 tbsp dried Italian herbs
- few sprigs of fresh thyme
- a handful of fresh basil leaves
- 1 small cauliflower, broken into small pieces or finely cut in a food processor or with a hand blender

1. Heat the olive oil in a large saucepan and add the mince, onions and garlic and cook for 5 minutes until the onions are soft and the mince is cooked.
2. Add the carrots, celery and peppers to the mix, stir and cook for another 5 minutes.
3. Add the tomatoes, tomato purée, sun-dried tomato paste and the herbs and stir.
4. Cover and simmer, stirring occasionally, for 1 hour.

INDONESIAN BEEF STEW

This Indonesian beef stew is slightly spicy. It is quick to prepare and tastes delicious.

Serves 4

Nutritional value:
Carbohydrates: 2
Protein portion: 1

Tip:
This dish goes well with red cabbage (see p94 for recipe), fresh beans or iceberg lettuce.

- 500g diced braising steak
- 100g onion, roughly chopped
- 1 tsp freshly ground black or white pepper
- 1 tsp ground nutmeg
- 1 tsp ground mace
- 2 tsp Himalayan salt
- 250ml water (use more if necessary)
- 50ml soy sauce (unsweetened)
- juice of half a lemon
- balsamic vinegar
- pure liquid Stevia

1. Put all the ingredients – except for the lemon juice, balsamic vinegar and Stevia – in a large frying pan, bring to the boil and heat on a low setting for 45-60 minutes, until the sauce becomes thick and the meat is cooked.
2. Add balsamic vinegar to taste and, if necessary, add Stevia.
3. Before serving sprinkle with lemon juice.

Serves 4

Nutritional value:
Carbohydrates: 10
Protein portion: 1
Vegetable portion: 1

LAMB FILLETS WITH ASPARAGUS & TOMATOES

- 24 cherry vine tomatoes or 6 vine tomatoes (halved and pips and juice removed)
- 4 garlic cloves, finely chopped
- 1 tbsp dried ground oregano
- 1 tbsp flat leaf parsley, finely chopped
- 3 tbsp olive oil
- 600g asparagus tips
- 400g lamb fillet
- freshly ground black pepper and Himalayan salt

1. Heat the oven to 180°C/350°F/Gas mark 4.
2. Mix the oregano, garlic and the flat leaf parsley. Scatter this mixture over the tomatoes, place the tomatoes on a grill tray, brush with olive oil, and bake in the oven for 15 minutes until squishy.
3. Place the asparagus in an oven proof dish, sprinkle with 1 tbsp of olive oil and cook in the oven for 10 minutes.
4. Season the lamb fillets with the pepper and salt, heat 1 tbsp olive oil in a medium size, non-stick frying pan and fry on a medium heat for 5 minutes on either side.
5. Remove the asparagus from the oven, arrange them on plates and serve with the roasted vine tomatoes and the cut lamb fillets.
6. Really nice with mint sauce (for recipe see page 34).

LAMB RAGOUT

Serves 4

Nutritional value:
Carbohydrates: 3½
Protein portion: 1½

Note:
One of my
favourites!

- 750g diced lamb leg steak or shoulder of lamb, discarding any fat or bones
- 3 garlic cloves, finely chopped
- the leaves from 4 sprigs of rosemary, washed and finely chopped
- 4 tbsp olive oil
- 4 tbsp tomato purée (paste)
- 375ml organic beef stock (made with ¾ stock cube)
- pinch each of Himalayan salt and freshly ground black pepper

1. Heat the oil in a non-stick frying pan and brown the meat on all sides over a medium heat.
2. Pour off excess fat.
3. Add the garlic and rosemary.
4. Stir the tomato purée (paste) into the beef stock and pour over the meat.
5. Season the meat with salt and pepper.
6. Cover and simmer, stirring occasionally, for 45-60 minutes until the meat is tender.

Tip: A freshly-made tomato salad goes well with this; or serve with French beans or a salad.

LEEK & MINCE BAKE

Serves 4

Nutritional value:

Carbohydrates: 5½

Protein portion: 1½

Vegetable portion: 1

- 400g leeks, trimmed and cut into small rings
- 250g mushrooms, thinly sliced
- 50g onion, finely chopped
- 2 large free range (organic) eggs
- 120g low fat grated cheese
- 400g lean (organic) minced beef (5% fat)
- Himalayan salt and freshly ground black pepper
- 3 tbsp fresh thyme

1. Preheat the oven 200°C/400°F/Gas mark 6.
2. Heat a large frying pan, add the minced beef and cook, stirring, for 5 minutes or until the beef is brown, discard any surplus fat.
3. Add the onion, mushrooms, leeks, herbs and salt and pepper to taste and cook, stirring, for 5 minutes.
4. When the vegetables are softened, add half the grated cheese and stir in one egg.
5. Arrange the mixture in a buttered oven proof dish, whisk the second egg and pour over the mixture.
6. Sprinkle with the rest of the grated cheese and bake in the oven for 30-35 minutes or until cooked.

Tips: • Serve with a nice fresh salad.
- This is an excellent family dish that can be enjoyed by all.

HEALTHY LASAGNE

Serves 8

Nutritional value:
Carbohydrates: 13½
Protein portion: 2
Vegetable portion: 2

- 2 tbsp olive oil
- 1kg lean (organic) minced beef (5% fat)
- 2 medium size onions, chopped
- 4 garlic cloves, crushed
- 2 x 400g cans chopped organic tomatoes
- 300ml beef stock made with ½ organic beef stock cubes
- ½ tube/50g tomato purée
- 1 tube/80g sun-dried tomato purée
- 1 tbsp of dried oregano
- 1 tbsp of dried basil
- Himalayan salt and freshly ground black pepper
- 2 courgettes, thinly sliced lengthways
- 1 jar of roasted red peppers in brine

For the cheese sauce:
- 500ml (organic) skimmed milk
- good grating of nutmeg or 1 tsp ground nutmeg
- Himalayan salt and freshly ground black pepper
- 3 tbsp cornflour
- 1 tsp of mustard
- 80g low fat, mature Cheddar cheese

1. **Make the meat sauce:** in a large frying pan heat the oil, add the beef, and cook on a medium heat, stirring, until browned.
2. Add the stock, tomatoes, onions, garlic, tomato purée, oregano, basil and salt and pepper to taste, and bring to the boil. Cover and simmer, stirring occasionally, for 1 hour.
3. Preheat the oven to 180°C/350°F/Gas mark 4.
4. Heat a griddle pan.
5. Season the courgettes and lightly chargrill or sear on each side, then leave on a plate until assembling time.
6. Drain the peppers and also add to the plate.
7. **Make the cheese sauce:** gently heat the milk with a good grating of nutmeg, some salt and pepper.
8. Mix the cornflour with 50ml of the milk and whisk back into the milk, bring to the boil, stirring constantly until the mixture thickens. Simmer for 2 to 3 minutes.
9. Add the mustard and half the cheese. Check the seasoning and set aside.
10. Take a large shallow ovenproof dish and start layering up the ingredients.
11. Start with a layer of meat, then peppers, then meat, then courgettes and finally cheese sauce.
12. Top with the rest of the cheese and bake in the oven for 20-30 minutes or until bubbling.

MINCED BEEF PIZZA

Serves 4

Nutritional value:
Carbohydrates: 5½
Protein portion: 2
Vegetable portion: 1

- 500g lean (organic) minced beef 5% fat
- 2 large free range (organic) eggs
- 120g low fat cheese, grated
- 8 slices of smoked meat or fish of your choice
- 4 tbsp tomato purée
- 1 tbps cold water
- 200g leeks, trimmed and thinly sliced

- 250g mushrooms, sliced
- 125g large red or yellow pepper, cored, seeded and cut into thin strips
- 100g onions, finely chopped
- 2 garlic cloves, crushed
- 2 tbsp dried Italian herbs
- Himalayan salt and freshly ground black pepper

1. Preheat the oven to 180°C/350°F/Gas mark 4.
2. In a bowl mix the mince with the eggs, 1 tbsp of Italian herbs, and salt and pepper to taste.
3. Grease a deep baking tray (size 22 x 29cm) and line with baking paper.
4. Press the mince down in the tray and make it as thin as possible so you can nearly see the bottom of the tray.
5. Bake in the oven for 15 minutes and pour off any excess fat and liquid.
6. In a bowl mix the tomato purée with water, salt, pepper, 1 tbsp Italian herbs (more if you want) and garlic until smooth.
7. Spread the tomato mixture over the mince meat.
8. Top with your choice of meat or fish.
9. Cover with the leeks, mushrooms, pepper and onions, and sprinkle with the grated cheese.
10. Bake in the oven for another 15-20 minutes.
11. Serve with a fresh green salad.

MOROCCAN
LAMB CUTLETS

Serves 4

Nutritional value:
Carbohydrates: 1½
Proteins: 100g lamb
is 1 protein portion

Tip:
Simple, quick and
very tasty.

- 1 tbsp olive oil
- ½ tsp ground cinnamon
- ½ tsp ground cumin
- ½ tsp ground coriander
- ½ tsp turmeric
- 8 lamb cutlets
- ½ bunch fresh coriander, finely chopped
- 1 lemon cut into quarters

1. Make a paste with the oil, cinnamon, cumin, coriander and turmeric.
2. Brush both sides of the cutlets with the oil mixture.
3. Lay the cutlets on the barbecue or under the grill and cook for around 6-7 minutes on either side.
4. Once cooked sprinkle with the fresh coriander.
5. Serve with the lemon.

MOUSSAKA

Serves 4

Nutritional value:

Carbohydrates: 15
Protein portion: 1½
Vegetable portion: 2½

Tip:
This moussaka
is made
without potatoes.

- 2 large aubergines, sliced
- 500g lean (organic) minced lamb
- 3 onions, roughly chopped
- 3 garlic cloves, crushed
- 680ml passatta
- 4 tbsp tomato purée
- 2 tsp dried oregano
- olive oil for brushing
- Himalayan salt and freshly ground black pepper
- ¼ of a bunch flat leaf parsley, chopped to garnish

Cheese sauce:

- 500ml (organic) skimmed milk
- A good grating of whole nutmeg or 1 tsp ground nutmeg
- Himalayan salt and freshly ground black pepper
- 3 tbsp cornflour
- 1 tsp of mustard
- 80g mature light Cheddar cheese

1. Preheat the oven to 180°C/350°F/Gas mark 4.
2. Arrange the aubergine slices into a colander, sprinkle generously with salt, and leave to stand for 30 minutes.
3. Heat a large frying pan on a medium heat, add the minced lamb and heat gently until the fat runs. Then increase the heat and cook, stirring, until browned. Spoon off any excess fat.
4. Add the onions and garlic and cook until softened.
5. Add the passatta, tomato purée, oregano, and salt and pepper to taste, and bring to the boil. Cover and simmer, stirring occasionally, for 20 minutes.
6. Rinse the aubergine slices and pat dry with paper towels.
7. Place on a grill rack and brush with the oil. Cook under a hot grill, 10cm from the heat, for 5-6 minutes until golden on both sides.
8. **Make the cheese sauce:** in a saucepan gently heat the milk with a good grating of nutmeg, some salt and pepper.
9. Mix the cornflour with 50ml of the milk and whisk back into the milk, bring to the boil, stirring constantly until the mixture thickens. Simmer for 2 to 3 minutes.
10. Add the mustard and cheese to the sauce and check the seasoning.
11. Spoon half of the meat mixture into a shallow ovenproof dish and top with half the aubergine slices. Repeat with the remaining meat and aubergines, finely pour over the cheese sauce.
12. Cook in the oven for 45 minutes or until golden.

PIZZA TOAST

A quick and healthy alternative to ready-made pizza.

Serves 1

Nutritional value:
Carbohydrates: 15
Protein portion: 1½
Vegetable portion: ⅓

Tip:
Nice with a fresh, green mixed salad.

- 1 slice of toasted wholemeal or spelt bread
- 2 tbsp tomato purée
- 6 green or black olives, cut in half
- ¼ of a large red pepper, cored, seeded and cut into thin strips
- 3 chestnut mushrooms, thinly sliced
- 40g Prosciutto ham, pastrami or cooked chicken, torn into strips
- 15g low fat cheese, grated
- 1 tbsp oregano or Italian herbs

1. Pre-heat the oven to 180°C/350°F/Gas mark 4.
2. Spread the tomato purée on the toasted bread.
3. Top with the mushrooms, pepper strips and olives.
4. Scatter the meat pieces over the toast.
5. Sprinkle with grated cheese.
6. Add oregano or Italian herbs to taste.
7. Place in a small ovenproof dish and heat in the oven until the cheese is melted.

CHAPTER 6

VEGETABLES & SALADS

CHICKEN SALAD WITH AVOCADO

Serves 1

Nutritional value:
Carbohydrates: 10
Protein portion: 1
Vegetable portion: 1

Tip:
Quick, simple
and delicious!

- 100g mixed lettuce leaves
- 100g cooked or roasted chicken, cut or torn into pieces
- 10 cherry tomatoes
- ½ ripe avocado
- 1 tbsp dried Italian herbs
- 2 tbsp extra virgin olive oil
- 1 tbsp balsamic vinegar
- 2 drops of pure liquid Stevia

1. Arrange the lettuce leaves on a large serving plate.
2. Decorate with the cherry tomatoes.
3. Arrange the chicken over the salad.
4. Cut the avocado in half lengthwise, through to the stone.
5. Twist the halves and then pull them apart.
6. Embed the blade of a sharp knife into the stone and lift it out.
7. Remove the skin and thinly slice half the avocado.
8. Arrange the slices on the lettuce leaves.
9. **Make the dressing:** in a small bowl whisk together the olive oil, balsamic vinegar, Italian herbs and the Stevia and drizzle over the salad.

ASPARAGUS WITH PAK CHOI AND RED PEPPER

LD

Serves 6

Nutritional value:

Carbohydrates: 10

Vegetable portion: 1

Tip:

A surprisingly great combination which goes really well with salmon.

- 500g asparagus spears, snapped to remove the hard ends, cut into 5cm pieces and blanched for 2 minutes
- 1 large or 2 small pak choi, washed and roughly cut
- 1 red chilli pepper, cut in half lengthwise, stalks and seeds removed, cut into thin strips
- 2 tbsp olive oil
- 1 tbsp soy sauce (unsweetened)
- Himalayan salt and freshly ground black pepper

1. Heat the olive oil on a medium heat in a wok or large frying pan, add the asparagus spears and stir-fry for 2 minutes.
2. Add the pak choi and the red pepper and stir-fry for 3 minutes.
3. Add the soy sauce and cook until the asparagus spears are tender.
4. Add pepper and Himalayan salt to taste.

"BALKAN" SALAD

Serves 6

Nutritional value:
Carbohydrates: 6
Protein portion: ⅓
Raw vegetable
portion: 1½

Note:
A lovely salad made
with feta cheese, a
creamy white Greek
cheese traditionally
made from ewes'
and goats' milk.
It has quite a
salty flavour.

- 1 large red, 1 large green and 1 large yellow pepper, cored, seeded and cut into 1cm squares
- ½ large cucumber, washed
- 1 large beef tomato or 2 medium sized tomatoes, cut into 1cm squares
- 1-2 garlic cloves, crushed
- 200g feta cheese, cut into 1cm squares
- Himalayan salt
- freshly ground black pepper
- 1 tbsp balsamic vinegar
- 1½ tbsp olive oil

1. Put the peppers into a large salad bowl, add a little salt and mix well. Leave to stand for 2 hours so the peppers become soft.
2. Cut the cucumber lengthwise. Remove the seeds with a teaspoon. Cut into 1cm squares.
3. Add the cucumber to the peppers and mix well.
4. Add the garlic and tomatoes to the pepper and cucumber mix.
5. Add the feta cheese to the mixture.
6. Season with pepper, salt, vinegar and the olive oil.
7. Mix well and leave to stand for half an hour.

Tip: This salad can be kept in the fridge for 2 weeks.

BALSAMIC MUSHROOMS

Serves 2

Nutritional value:
Carbohydrates: 6
Vegetable portion: 1

Tip:
This dish is perfect
as a starter or
snack served on
wholemeal toast or
oatcakes.

- 400g chestnut mushrooms, cleaned and quartered
- 1 small red chilli pepper, cored, seeded and finely chopped (or use 2 tsp chilli powder)
- 3 tbsp olive oil
- 2 shallots, finely chopped
- 2 garlic cloves, finely chopped
- 4 tbsp balsamic vinegar
- 1-2 tbsp white wine vinegar
- 15 drops pure liquid Stevia
- 2 tbsp flat leaf parsley, finely chopped
- Himalayan salt and freshly ground black pepper

1. Heat the olive oil in a wok or frying pan and fry the shallots for 2-3 minutes until soft.
2. Add the garlic and chilli pepper and fry for 2 more minutes.
3. Then add the mushrooms and fry on a high heat for another 2 minutes.
4. Turn the heat down and pour the balsamic and white wine vinegar into the pan, add the Stevia and cook on a low heat for 10-15 minutes.
5. Add pepper and salt and more Stevia if necessary.
6. Garnish with the parsley.

CAESAR SALAD

- 3 garlic cloves, squashed with the blade of a knife and skinned
- 175ml extra virgin olive oil
- 2 slices of old wholemeal bread
- 3-4 Cos lettuces
- Himalayan salt and freshly ground black pepper
- 60ml freshly squeezed lemon juice

- 2 tbsp homemade mayonnaise (p33) or ready-made mayonnaise without sugar
- 6 chopped anchovy fillets
- 1 hard boiled large, free range (organic) egg
- 100g hard goat's or parmesan cheese

1. Preheat the oven to 150°C/300°F/Gas mark 2.
2. Put the garlic in a small bowl and cover with the olive oil.
3. Marinate for 1 hour.
4. Chop the egg into quarters lengthwise.
5. Cut the bread into 2cm squares.
6. Remove the garlic from the oil and discard.
7. Drizzle the bread squares with 4 tbsp of the garlic flavoured oil and bake in the preheated oven for 20 minutes, turning regularly.
8. Discard outer leaves of the lettuce.
9. Tear the leftover leaves into 5cm pieces and put them in a salad bowl.
10. Mix the salt, pepper, the leftover garlic oil, lemon juice and mayonnaise.
11. Pour this mixture over the lettuce leaves and mix carefully.
12. Add the anchovies and mix well.
13. Sprinkle with cheese of your choice.

LD

Serves 4

Nutritional value:
Carbohydrates: 8
Grain portion: ½
Protein portion: ½

CELERIAC PURÉE

This purée is starch free and an excellent alternative to potato purée. It can be made ahead of time.

Tip:
Blend in the fresh horseradish to taste – much depends on your taste buds and the fiery strength of the root.

To re-heat put the celeriac purée in a saucepan and heat gently, without boiling, adding a splash of water if necessary to stop it burning.

Serves 4–6

Nutritional value:
Carbohydrates: 10
Protein portion: ¼
Vegetable portion: 1½

- 3 tbsp of olive oil
- 2 onions, finely chopped
- 4 cloves of garlic, crushed
- Himalayan salt and freshly ground black pepper
- 1½kg celeriac, peeled and cut into cubes
- 300ml crème fraîche (see p30 for recipe)
- 4 tbsp Dijon or wholegrain mustard
- optional: 15cm piece of fresh horseradish, about the diameter of a £2 coin, peeled and grated (or 10-12 tbsp horseradish sauce)
- thyme leaves for scattering

1. Cover the celeriac with 1200ml water and bring to the boil.
2. Reduce the heat, cover and simmer for 30 minutes until tender.
3. Heat the olive oil in a large saucepan and add the onion and garlic. Cook gently for 5 minutes, until the onion is soft but not brown. Set aside.
4. When ready drain the celeriac and liquidise to a smooth purée with the crème fraîche and mustard.
5. Add the onions and garlic mixture to the purée.
6. Season to taste.
7. Serve in a bowl and scatter a few thyme leaves over the top.
8. You can keep the purée for a day in the fridge.

CHICKEN SALAD WITH OLIVES AND SUN-DRIED TOMATOES

Serves 1

Nutritional value:

Carbohydrates: 11

Protein portion: 1

Vegetable portion: 1½

Tips:

- Quick, simple and delicious!
- You can substitute the tomatoes and olives with cucumber and/or raw large peppers.

- 100g mixed lettuce leaves
- 100g cooked or roasted chicken, cut or torn into pieces
- 1 large tomato, sliced
- 7 sun-dried tomatoes
- 4 green olives
- 2 tbsp extra virgin olive oil
- 1 tbsp balsamic vinegar
- ½ tbsp dried Italian herbs
- 2 drops pure liquid Stevia

1. Arrange the lettuce leaves on a large serving plate.
2. Decorate with the tomato, sun-dried tomatoes and green olives.
3. Arrange the chicken over the salad.
4. Mix the olive oil, balsamic vinegar, Stevia and Italian herbs and drizzle over the salad.

COLESLAW WITH APPLE

Serves 4

Nutritional value:

Carbohydrates: 8

Protein portion: ¼

Vegetable portion: 1

Tip:

Add a few drops of pure liquid Stevia or freshly squeezed lemon juice to the dressing.

- 2 large carrots, grated
- ¼ of a medium size white cabbage (around 200g), finely shredded
- 10cm piece of cucumber, grated
- 8 small pickled onions, finely chopped
- ½ apple, grated
- 6 tbsp plain fat-free Greek yoghurt (0%)
- ½ tsp mustard
- freshly ground black pepper and Himalayan salt

1. Put the carrots, white cabbage, cucumber, pickled onions and apple into a large bowl.
2. Make the dressing: combine the yoghurt, mustard, and add salt and pepper to taste.
3. Pour the dressing over the salad and toss gently.
4. Cover and leave to chill for 1 hour.
5. Taste the coleslaw for seasoning and serve.

RED CABBAGE

Serves 4

Nutritional value:
Carbohydrates: 2
Vegetable portion: 1

- 1 red cabbage weighing 900g
- 3 tbsp olive oil
- 3 tbsp balsamic vinegar
- 12-15 drops pure liquid Stevia

1. Cut the cabbage into quarters, remove the white hard stem and finely shred each quarter.

2. Heat the olive oil in a large sauce pan, add the cabbage and cook stirring occasionally. Make sure the oil does not burn.

3. Add in the balsamic vinegar and Stevia.

4. Cover and cook over a low heat for 30 minutes or until the cabbage is tender but still firm. If there is too much liquid, uncover, and boil rapidly until the liquid has evaporated completely.

The red cabbage can be eaten in other ways as well:

Stir-fry until the cabbage is hot and still fairly crisp.

Stewed; cook the cabbage on a low heat until soft. The taste can be made more intense by adding more balsamic vinegar and/or Stevia.

COURGETTE SALAD
WITH FRESH MINT

LD

Serves 4

Nutritional value:

Carbohydrates: 4

Vegetable portion: 1

Tip:

Serve with fish or
with meat from
the barbecue.

- 400g courgettes, washed and cut into ½cm slices
- 2 garlic cloves, crushed
- 2 tbsp extra virgin olive oil
- handful of fresh mint leaves, finely cut
- 1½ tbsp white wine / balsamic vinegar
- freshly ground black pepper
- Himalayan salt

1. Pat the courgette slices dry with kitchen towel.
2. Heat 1 tbsp of the olive oil in wok or a frying pan, add the courgettes and stir-fry for 3-4 minutes until the courgettes are just beginning to colour.
3. Remove the courgettes from the pan and place them in a large mixing bowl.
4. Sprinkle the garlic and mint over the courgettes.
5. Add the vinegar and salt and pepper to taste.
6. Drizzle with the rest of the olive oil and mix it all together.
7. Leave to stand for a few hours to enhance the taste.

PEPPER SALAD WITH RED ONION AND BEAN SPROUTS

Serves 4

Nutritional value:

Carbohydrates: 5

Vegetable portion: 1

Variation:

You can also fry the bean sprouts with the pepper and onions or even add the onions raw after having cooked the peppers.

- 2 tbsp oilve oil
- 2 red onions cut into thin rings
- 200g bean sprouts
- 1 red, 1 green and 1 yellow pepper, cored, seeded and cut into strips
- 1 large garlic clove, crushed
- 2 tbsp soy sauce (unsweetened)
- 1 tbsp fresh lime juice
- freshly ground black pepper and Himalayan salt

1. Heat the olive oil in a frying pan, add the pepper and onions.
2. After 2½ minutes add the crushed garlic and fry for a further 2½ minutes on a medium heat.
3. Remove the pepper and onion mixture from the pan and let it cool down.
4. Add the bean sprouts, soy sauce and lime juice, mix well.
5. Add pepper and salt to taste.

CUCUMBER SALAD

Serves 4

Nutritional value:
Carbohydrates: 9½
Fruit portion: ¾
Protein portion: ½
Raw vegetable
portion: 2

- 4 celery stalks, cut into thin strips
- 1 cucumber, peeled and cut into thin strips
- 1 apple, peeled and cut into thin strips
- 1-2 tbsp extra virgin olive oil
- juice of half a lemon
- 150g goat's cheese
- freshly ground black pepper and Himalayan salt
- handful of celery leaves, chopped

1. Put the celery, cucumber and apple in a large salad bowl and mix with the olive oil and lemon juice.
2. Crumble the goat's cheese over the salad.
3. Add pepper and salt to taste.
4. Garnish with the chopped celery leaves.

Tips: Use mild goat's cheese so the taste of the cucumber and celery will not be overwhelmed.

MACKEREL SALAD

LD

Serves 4

Nutritional value:
Carbohydrates: 6
Protein portion: 1
Vegetable portion: 1

Note:
Full of omega 3 and
quick to make.

- 100g mixed lettuce leaves
- 150g steamed or smoked mackerel
- 4 slices of cucumber
- 2 radishes, sliced
- 1 tbsp mayonnaise (homemade p33) or ready-made without sugar
- Himalayan salt and freshly ground black pepper

1. Arrange the lettuce leaves on a large serving plate.
2. Arrange the mackerel on top of the lettuce leaves.
3. Decorate the salad with the cucumber and radishes.
4. Drizzle with mayonnaise.
5. Add salt and pepper to taste.

MOZZARELLA AND AVOCADO SALAD

Serves 1

Nutritional value:

Carbohydrates: 8

Protein portion: 1

Vegetable portion: 1

Tip:

This salad can also be served without the lettuce; use one small beef tomato instead of the small tomatoes and arrange on a plate.

- 100g mixed lettuce leaves
- 6 small vine tomatoes
- ½ avocado, cut into thin slices
- 60g mozzarella light cheese, cut into slices
- 1 tsp dried Italian herbs
- 1½ tbsp extra virgin olive oil
- ½ tbsp balsamic vinegar
- 4 drops pure liquid Stevia
- freshly ground black pepper and Himalayan salt

1. Arrange the lettuce leaves on a large serving plate.
2. Add the tomatoes, avocado and mozzarella.
3. Make the dressing: combine the Italian herbs, olive oil, balsamic vinegar, Stevia, pepper and salt to taste.

FRESH GREENS

Serves 4

Nutritional value:
Carbohydrates: 3
Vegetable portion: 1

Note:
Really tasty!

- 500g fresh greens
- 1 tsp ground ginger
- ½ vegetable stock cube
- 1 tsp chilli powder
- 1 tbsp soy sauce (unsweetened)
- 2 tbsp olive oil
- 1 onion, finely chopped
- 1 garlic clove, crushed

1. Take the greens, cut away the stalks and shred the leaves.
2. Wash thoroughly.
3. Heat the olive oil in a wok or large frying pan.
4. Add the onion, crushed garlic, ginger and chilli powder and stir-fry over a high heat for about 2-3 minutes until the onion is beginning to brown.
5. Crumble the stock cube and add to the onion mixture.
6. Add the shredded greens and stir-fry over a medium high heat for 4-5 minutes until softened.
7. Finally add the soy sauce.

Tip: Goes really well with spicy chicken (see page 64, for recipe).

QUICK RATATOUILLE

Serves 4

Nutritional value:

Carbohydrates: 10

Vegetable portion: 1½

Tip:

This can be a most attractive dish but not if it ends up mushy. So to avoid this, make sure you don't cut up the vegetables too small (they must retain their individuality). Goes well with chicken, fish or meat balls.

- 2 large aubergines, cut into 1cm square chunks
- 3 courgettes, thinly sliced
- 1 onion, sliced
- 1 large red pepper, cored, seeded and cut into 2cm chunks
- 2 tbsp olive oil
- 2 tbsp fresh or dried thyme
- 1 tin of chopped (organic) tomatoes
- freshly ground black pepper and Himalayan salt

1. Heat the olive oil in a large frying pan and add the aubergines, courgettes, onion and pepper.
2. Cook on a medium heat, while stirring, for about 5 minutes.
3. Add the thyme and chopped tomatoes.
4. Add pepper and salt to taste.
5. Cook gently, covered for 20 minutes until the vegetables are soft but still retain their shape (see tip).

SAMPHIRE WITH GARLIC AND LEMON

Serves 4

Nutritional value:

Carbohydrates: 4

Vegetable portion: 1

Tip:

Samphire, a super food and also known as sea-asparagus, is easy to prepare and tastes delicious. Serve it with any type of fish.

- 350g fresh samphire
- juice of ½ lemon
- 1-2 garlic cloves, finely chopped
- 2 tbsp extra virgin olive oil

1. Trim the samphire to remove the tough woody parts of the lower stalks and give it a light wash to remove any grit.

2. Cook the samphire in boiling water for 2-3 minutes or until just tender. Drain.

3. Cool the samphire with iced water and set aside in a serving bowl.

4. In a small bowl combine the olive oil, chopped garlic, lemon juice and drizzle over the samphire. Mix well.

TUNA SALAD

Serves 1

Nutritional value:

Carbohydrates: 5

Protein portion: 1

Vegetable portion: 1

Tip:

Simple, quick and very tasty.

- 100g mixed lettuce leaves
- 150g tuna in spring water
- 6-8 cherry tomatoes, cut in half
- 2-3 spring onions, finely chopped
- 2 tbsp of extra virgin olive oil
- 1 tsp balsamic vinegar
- 6 drops of pure liquid Stevia
- Himalayan salt and freshly ground black pepper

1. Arrange the lettuce leaves on a large serving plate.
2. Drain the tuna, coarsely flake it with a fork and place on the lettuce.
3. Arrange the tomatoes and spring onions over the tuna.
4. Make the dressing by combining the olive oil, balsamic vinegar and Stevia, and add salt and pepper to taste. Drizzle over the salad.

SMOKED SALMON SALAD

Serves 1

Nutritional value:

Carbohydrates: 6
Protein portion: 1
Vegetable portion: 1

- 100g mixed lettuce leaves
- 7 cherry tomatoes
- 100g smoked salmon
- 1½ tbsp extra virgin olive oil
- 1 tsp balsamic vinegar
- freshly ground black pepper to taste

1. Arrange the lettuce leaves on a large serving plate.
2. Mix the olive oil with the balsamic vinegar and drizzle over the lettuce leaves, mix well.
3. Add pepper to taste.
4. Arrange the salmon on top of the lettuce leaves.
5. Decorate the salad with the cherry tomatoes.

LD

Serves 4

Nutritional value:
Carbohydrates: 10
Protein portion: ¾
Vegetable portion: 1

SPICY BRUSSELS SPROUTS

To be honest, I did not like Brussels sprouts very much as they are often overcooked and taste floury. However, this recipe changed my mind.

- 400g Brussels sprouts
- 2 tbsp of olive oil
- 1 red onion, finely chopped
- 2 garlic cloves, crushed
- 1 tsp chilli powder

- 11g plant based protein powder
- 200g cottage cheese
- Himalayan salt and freshly ground black pepper
- 1 tbsp finely chopped fresh rosemary
- 60g low fat cheese, grated

1. Preheat the oven to 180°C/350°F/Gas mark 4.
2. Boil 1 litre of water, add the sprouts and simmer for 3-4 minutes until just tender.
3. Drain and put them on a plate.
4. Heat the olive oil in a frying pan, add the onion and garlic and cook gently on a medium heat for 5 minutes or until lightly browned.
5. Add the chilli and protein powder and fry for a further minute.
6. Add the cottage cheese and mix well. Bring the mixture to the boil.
7. Add salt and pepper to taste.
8. Stir in the rosemary and the sprouts.
9. Arrange the vegetable mixture in an oven proof dish and sprinkle with the grated cheese.
10. Place in the oven and cook for 25 minutes.

ASPARAGUS THE FLEMISH WAY

Serves 4

Nutritional value:
Carbohydrates: 8
Protein portion: 1½
Vegetable portion: 1

- 6 hard boiled free range (organic) eggs
- 600g asparagus
- 2 tbsp flat leaf parsley, finely cut
- 80g unsalted real butter (± 4 tbsps)
- juice of half a lemon
- freshly ground black pepper and Himalayan salt

1. Clean the asparagus and snap off the tough part of the stalk.
2. In a large pan bring 1½ litres of water to the boil.
3. Carefully add the asparagus to the boiling water and return to the boil. Simmer for 4-5 minutes until tender. You can also steam or microwave the asparagus.
4. Divide them over 4 plates.
5. Melt the butter in a small pan and add the lemon juice.
6. Add pepper and salt to taste.
7. Shell the eggs and mash them with a fork.
8. Mix in the flat leaf parsley and some pepper.
9. Pour the melted butter over the asparagus and garnish with the egg mixture.
10. Serve immediately.

CHAPTER 7

EGG &
VEGETARIAN DISHES

AUBERGINE AND SPINACH BAKE

Serves 4

Nutritional value:

Carbohydrates
per 100g: 5
Protein portion: ¾
Vegetable portion: 1

Tip:
Serve with a nice
tomato salad.

- 1 small aubergine, cut into small cubes
- 100g courgette, cut into thin slices
- 1 red onion, cut into rings
- 200g fresh spinach, washed and roughly chopped
- 60g parmesan cheese, grated
- 120g ricotta cheese
- 100ml vegetable stock (¼ stock cube)
- 1 tbsp olive oil
- freshly ground black pepper and Himalayan salt

1. Preheat oven to 220°C/450°F/Gas mark 8.
2. Mix the ricotta cheese with the stock and add pepper and salt to taste. Set aside.
3. Heat the olive oil in a large frying pan, add the aubergine, courgette and onion and fry, stirring for 5-10 minutes until the onions are soft but not burned.
4. Add the spinach and cook for another 2 minutes.
5. Transfer the vegetables to an oven proof dish and cover with the ricotta stock mixture.
6. Sprinkle with the parmesan cheese and bake in the oven for about 10 minutes until golden.

AUBERGINE "MUFFINS"

- 1 aubergine, cut lengthways into ¾cm thick slices
- 5 tbsp olive oil
- 1 small courgette, cut into 1cm square cubes
- 1 garlic clove, finely chopped
- 2 roasted red peppers from a jar (without sugar), finely cut
- 30g sun-dried tomatoes from a jar (without sugar) finely cut
- 1 large free range (organic) egg
- 4 sprigs of basil, leaves only
- freshly ground black pepper and Himalayan salt

You will need a griddle pan and a muffin tin, greased.

1. Pre-heat the oven to 200°C/400°F/ Gas mark 6.
2. Brush the aubergine slices with the olive oil.
3. Heat the griddle pan and grill the aubergine slices on high for 1-2 minutes.
4. Halfway through turn them over and once cooked let them cool down.
5. Heat 2 tbsp olive oil in a frying pan, add the courgettes and garlic and cook gently for 5 minutes or until just tender.
6. Add salt and pepper to taste.
7. Take the pan off the heat and add the peppers, tomatoes and egg and mix well.

Assemble the muffins:

8. Cover 8 muffin moulds with the aubergine slices and let them hang over the sides.
9. Fill the moulds with the courgette mixture and cover with the aubergine slices.
10. Bake the aubergine muffins in the oven for 15-20 minutes or until golden brown.
11. When cooked take the muffins out by putting a plate on top of the tray and turn over (2 muffins weigh about 125g)
12. Drizzle with the olive oil and garnish with the basil leaves.

SLD

Serves 4

Nutritional value for 2 muffins:
Carbohydrates: 4
Protein portion: ¼
Vegetable portion: 1

CHEESE OMELETTE

Serves 1

Nutritional value:
Protein portion: 2½

Tip:
An ideal dish for any time of the day.

- 2 large free range (organic) eggs
- 30g low fat cheese, grated
- 1 tbsp Italian dried herbs, dill or chives
- freshly ground black pepper
- Himalayan salt
- 1 tbsp olive oil

1. Beat or whisk the eggs, herbs, pepper and salt together in a large bowl until light and fluffy.
2. Heat the oil in a non-stick frying pan and pour in the eggs.
3. Cook over a medium heat.
4. As the eggs begin to set, lift and pull back the edge of the omelette, tilting the pan so liquid egg can run to the side of the pan.
5. Continue cooking until the omelette is just set and the underside is golden brown.
6. Sprinkle cheese on half of the omelette. Loosen the edge and with a palette knife, lift the uncovered half of the omelette and flip it over the filling.
7. Slide on to a warmed plate and serve.

CLEAR MUSHROOM SOUP

Serves 4

Nutritional value:

Carbohydrates: 2½

Vegetable portion: ½

- 450g fresh mushrooms, cleaned and cut into small pieces
- 15g dried mushrooms
- 1 onion, finely chopped
- 3 garlic cloves, crushed
- 2 tbsp olive oil
- 1 litre organic vegetable (or chicken) stock
- 1 tsp lemon juice
- 2-3 tbsp chopped fresh thyme
- 2-3 tbsp chopped fresh flat leaf parsley
- freshly ground black pepper
- soy sauce (unsweetened)

1. Soak the dried mushrooms in water for 30 minutes. Drain, but keep the water and set aside.
2. Heat the olive oil in a large saucepan, add the onion and garlic, and cook gently, stirring occasionally, for a few minutes until soft but not coloured.
3. Add the fresh and dried mushrooms and cook on a medium heat, stirring from time to time, for 10 minutes.
4. Add the stock, the mushroom water, the thyme, 2 tbsp of the parsley, and salt and pepper to taste and bring to a boil, cover, and simmer gently for 10 minutes.
5. Add the lemon juice and soy sauce.
6. Taste for seasoning.
7. Serve the soup hot and garnish with the remaining parsley.

COURGETTE FRITTATA

Serves 2

**Nutritional value
per slice:**

Carbohydrates: 1½

Protein portion: 1

Vegetable portion: ⅓

Tips:

• You can use this
recipe as a snack or
serve for lunch.

• When cut into
small pieces,
they make
great canapés.

- 175g courgettes, thickly sliced
- 6 large free range (organic) eggs
- 2 tbsp olive oil
- 75g onion, finely chopped
- 1 garlic clove, finely chopped
- Himalayan salt and freshly ground black pepper

1. Preheat the grill to 180°C/350°F/Gas mark 5.
2. Blanch the courgettes in boiling water for about 3 minutes. Drain and rinse under cold running water.
3. Heat the olive oil in a non-stick, ovenproof frying pan.
4. Add the onion and garlic and cook for 1-2 minutes on a low heat.
5. Break the eggs into a bowl, add salt and pepper to taste and beat with a fork.
6. Add the courgettes to the onion and garlic in the frying pan, then pour over the eggs.
7. Cook over a low heat for about 10 minutes.
8. As the eggs set, lift the frittata with a spatula and tilt the pan to allow the uncooked egg to run underneath.
9. When the eggs are set, place the frying pan under the preheated grill, 10cm from the heat for 1-2 minutes until the top is golden brown and firm when pressed.
10. Cut the frittata into 6 wedges and serve hot or cold.

EGG PANCAKES WITH SPINACH

Serves 4

Nutritional value
per pancake:
Carbohydrates: 4½
Protein portion: 1
Vegetable portion: ½

- 1kg spinach leaves, coarsley chopped
- 125g extra light low fat cheese spread
- 120g Parmesan cheese, grated
- Himalayan salt and freshly ground black pepper
- large pinch of grated or ground nutmeg
- 4 large free range (organic) eggs
- 2 tbsp water
- 1 tbsp olive oil

1. Preheat the oven to 190°C/375°F/Gas mark 5
2. Rinse the spinach and put into a large saucepan with only the water that clings to the leaves. Cook for about 4-5 minutes until tender. Drain well, squeezing to extract as much water as you can. Spoon into a medium size bowl.
3. Stir in the low fat cheese spread and 60g Parmesan cheese and add salt, pepper and nutmeg to taste.
4. Break the eggs into a medium size bowl, add salt and pepper to taste, and beat in the water with a fork.
5. Heat a little olive oil in a small non-stick frying pan. When the oil is hot, pour 2 tbsp of the egg mixture into the pan.
6. Cook the eggs over a medium heat pulling back the edge as the eggs set and tilting the pan to allow the uncooked egg to run to the side of the pan. Continue until the eggs are lightly set and the underside is golden brown. Loosen and turn over until cooked.
7. Make 7 more pancakes in the same way.
8. Fill each pancake with 1 tbsp of the spinach mixture, roll it and put it in an oven proof dish. Lay the omelettes close together.
9. Sprinkle with the leftover Parmesan cheese
10. Bake in the oven for around 25 minutes.

EGG SPECIAL WITH VEGETABLES

Serves 2

Nutritional value:

Carbohydrates: 5

Grain portion
(slice of toast): 1, add
13 carbohydrates

Protein portion: 2

Vegetable portion: ½

- 1 tbsp olive oil
- ⅓ of a courgette, thinly sliced
- 8 mushrooms, thinly sliced
- Himalayan salt and freshly ground black pepper
- 1 tsp paprika powder
- 4 large free range (organic) eggs, whisked or beaten
- 2 tbsp crème fraîche
- 2 slices of spelt, wholemeal or sourdough bread to toast

1. Preheat the oven to 180°C/350°F/Gas mark 4.
2. Heat the oil in a non-stick frying pan, add the courgette and mushrooms with the salt, pepper and paprika powder and cook, stirring, for 1 minute or until softened.
3. Divide the vegetables between 2 small oven proof dishes and cover each with 2 eggs; or use one medium sized oven proof dish and cover with 4 eggs.
4. Mix the crème fraîche into the egg mixture.
5. Add pepper to taste and cook in the oven for 8 minutes until set and golden.
6. Serve with a slice of toast.

LEEK WITH NUTS AND TOMATOES

Serves 2

Nutritional value:

Vegetable: 1

Raw vegetable: 1

Carbohydrates: 15

Protein portion: 1

Tip:

This dish can be served as a salad or used as a filling for an omelette.

- 3 small leeks, white part only, cut into thick rings
- 60g hazelnuts, roasted and finely chopped
- 4 tomatoes, sliced
- ½-1 tbsp balsamic vinegar, depending on your taste
- Himalayan salt and freshly ground black pepper
- 2 tbsp olive oil

1. Divide the sliced tomatoes over two plates.
2. Heat 1 tbsp olive oil in a frying pan, add the leeks and fry, over a medium heat, for 4-5 minutes until the leeks are just beginning to colour.
3. Spread the leeks over the tomatoes.
4. Sprinkle with the balsamic vinegar and the rest of the olive oil.
5. Garnish with the hazelnuts.
6. Add salt and pepper to taste.

Omelette variation

The omelette is used as a base. Once the omelette is cooked on one side, turn it over and spread first the cooked leeks on the top then add the tomatoes, vinegar and hazelnuts.

PORTOBELLO CAPRESE

Serves 2

Nutritional value:
Carbohydrates: 5
Protein portion: ½
Vegetable portion: 1

Note:
A perfect starter.

- 4 portobello mushrooms, stalks removed and cut into small pieces
- 2 fresh medium sized tomatoes, sliced
- 8 sun-dried tomatoes
- 125g mozzarella cheese
- 1½ tbsp dried Italian herbs
- 12 basil leaves
- freshly ground black pepper and Himalayan salt

1. Preheat the oven to 180°C/350°F/Gas mark 4.
2. Cut the mozzarella cheese into 4 slices and cut the remainder into small pieces.
3. In a bowl, mix the mozzarella pieces with the cut up mushrooms stalks.
4. Add salt and pepper to taste.
5. Fill the portobello mushrooms with the mozzarella and mushroom mixture.
6. Put two sun-dried tomatoes and 3 basil leaves on each mushroom mixture and cover with a slice of tomato.
7. Finally cover with a slice of the mozzarella cheese.
8. Place the mushrooms in a shallow oven proof dish and cook in the oven for 15-20 minutes. Serve at once.

QUORN OR TOFU MINCE RATATOUILLE

LD

Serves 4

Nutritional value:

Carbohydrates: 5

Protein portion: 1½

Vegetable portion: 1

Tips:

• Other herbs you can use are oregano, basil or Italian herbs.

• Nice with iceberg lettuce.

- 180g quorn mince or minced tofu
- 200g mushrooms, cut into slices
- 50g onion, cut into rings
- 100g cucumber, cut into small cubes
- 60g low fat cheese, grated
- Himalayan salt and freshly ground black pepper
- fresh or dried herbs of your choice, like thyme or parsley
- 1 tbsp olive oil

1. Heat the olive oil in a frying pan, fry the mushrooms and onions for 5-6 minutes on a medium heat, until the onions are glazed but not brown.
2. Add the cucumber, mince, salt, pepper and herbs.
3. Mix well and fry for 3-4 minutes until cooked.
4. Sprinkle with the cheese and let the cheese melt, ideally using a fitted lid.

SMOKED SALMON & MOZZARELLA FRITTATA

Recipe courtesy of Mara Thorne.

- 120g smoked salmon, cut into very small pieces (or you can use a packet of "trimmings")
- 4 large free range (organic) eggs
- 6-8 mozzarella pearls, drained (or one mozzarella cut into cubes)
- 2 tsp of dried dill (or chopped fresh dill if you have it)
- splash of soya milk
- freshly ground black pepper and Himalayan salt if desired
- 1 tbsp of olive oil

1. Preheat the grill to 190°/375°/Gas mark 5.
2. Place the smoked salmon pieces into a large bowl and break in the eggs.
3. Beat with a splash of milk, the dill, pepper and salt to taste (don't add too much salt as the smoked salmon is salty).
4. Mix in the Mozzarella pearls but be careful not to break them up.
5. Heat the oil in a large non-stick, ovenproof frying pan, pour in the egg mixture
6. Cook over a medium heat for about 3-4 minutes. As the eggs set, lift the frittata with a spatula and tilt the pan to allow the uncooked egg to run underneath.
7. When the eggs are set place the frying pan under the grill, 10cm from the heat for another 3-4 minutes until the top is golden brown and firm when pressed and the Mozzarella has melted.
8. Serve at once, cut in half, on a warmed plate.

BS
LD

Serves 2

Nutritional value:
Protein portion: 2½

Tip:
Serve with a mixed salad, steamed broccoli or green beans.

STUFFED RED PEPPER

Serves 1

Nutritional value:

Carbohydrates: 10

Protein portion: 1

Vegetable portion: 1

- 3 spring onions, cut into small rings
- 1 tbsp fresh basil, finely chopped
- 1 tbsp fresh flat leaf parsley, finely chopped
- 1 tbsp olive oil
- 1 large red pepper, washed
- ¼ small onion, finely chopped
- 1 large garlic clove, skin removed
- 100g cottage cheese
- freshly ground black pepper
- Himalayan salt
- herbs of your choice, such as thyme or basil

You will need some kitchen foil

1. Preheat the oven to 200°C/400°F/Gas mark 6.
2. Heat the olive oil in a frying pan, on a medium heat, add the onion and fry until golden.
3. Place both the pepper and garlic clove onto a baking tray, place in the oven and cook for 20 minutes.
4. Once ready remove the garlic from the tray, cover the pepper with kitchen foil and set aside for 10 minutes.
5. In a bowl crush the garlic and mix with the cottage cheese, spring onions, basil, fried onion and parsley. Add salt and pepper to taste.
6. Remove the skin from the pepper and discard the cores, seeds, and white ribs.
7. Fill the pepper with the cottage cheese mixture and serve warm.

TOMATO SOUP

Serves 6-8

Nutritional value
100ml soup:
Carbohydrates: 12
Vegetable portion: 1

- 2 tbsp olive oil
- 2 onions, coarsely chopped
- 1 garlic clove, crushed
- 1 ¼ litres vegetable (or chicken) stock
- 2 x 400g cans organic chopped tomatoes
- 3 bay leaves
- Himalayan salt and freshly ground black pepper
- 4 tbsp ready made or homemade pesto (for recipe see page 31)
- fresh basil leaves to garnish

1. Heat the olive oil in a large saucepan, add the onions and garlic, and cook gently, stirring from time to time, for a few minutes until soft but not coloured.
2. Pour in the stock and add the tomatoes and their juice, the bay leaves and salt and pepper to taste. Bring to a boil, cover the pan, and simmer gently for 20 minutes.
3. Remove the bay leaves and discard. Purée the soup in a food processor or with a hand blender until smooth.
4. Return the soup to the pan, add the pesto, and heat through. Taste for seasoning.
5. Serve at once, garnished with basil leaves.

VEGETABLE FRITTATA

SLD

Serves 1

Nutritional value:

Carbohydrates: 9

Protein portion: 2½

Vegetable portion: 1¼

- 2 large free range (organic) eggs
- 1 small onion, finely cut
- 6 medium size mushrooms, cut into thin slices
- 6 cherry tomatoes, cut in half
- 50g cooked fresh spinach, finely chopped
- 30g low fat cheese, grated
- 1 tbsp Italian dried herbs
- freshly ground black pepper and Himalayan salt
- 1 tbsp olive oil

1. Preheat the grill to 180°C/350°F/Gas mark 5.
2. Heat the oil in a non-stick, ovenproof frying pan over a medium heat.
3. When hot, add the onion and mushrooms and cook, stirring, for 5 minutes or until softened.
4. Add the tomatoes and spinach and cook, stirring, for a further 2 minutes.
5. Beat or whisk the eggs, herbs, pepper and salt together in a large bowl until light and fluffy.
6. Pour the eggs over the vegetables and cook over a medium heat for about 8 minutes.
7. As the eggs begin to set, lift the frittata with a spatula and tilt the pan to allow the uncooked egg to run underneath.
8. When the eggs are set, sprinkle with cheese, and place the pan under a hot grill, 10cm from the heat, for 1-2 minutes until the top is golden brown and firm when pressed. Cut in half and slide on to a warmed plate and serve.

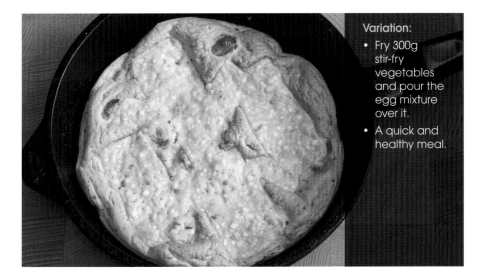

Variation:
- Fry 300g stir-fry vegetables and pour the egg mixture over it.
- A quick and healthy meal.

INDEX